Language, Literacy and Culture
School of Education
University of Colorado at Denver
1200 Larimer St. Campus Box 106
Denver, CO 80204-5300
(303) 556-4366

To Dominique, la bonne

Learning Purpose and Language Use

H. G. Widdowson

Oxford University Press
1983

Oxford University Press
Walton Street, Oxford OX2 6DP

London Glasgow New York
Toronto Delhi Bombay Calcutta Madras Karachi
Kuala Lumpur Singapore Hong Kong Tokyo
Nairobi Dar Es Salaam Cape Town
Melbourne Auckland

and associated companies in
Beirut Berlin Ibadan Mexico City Nicosia

OXFORD is a trade mark of Oxford University Press

ISBN 0 19 437072 0

Set in 10 pt Linotron Sabon by
Graphicraft Typesetters Limited, Hong Kong
Printed in Hong Kong.

Contents

Introduction 1

CHAPTER ONE Learning purpose 5

A Argument 5
B Discussion 14
    1. Historical perspectives 14
    2. Education and training 16
    3. Aims, objectives, and learner needs 20
    4. Competence and capacity 23
    5. Register analysis and needs analysis 28
    6. Restricted languages 29
    7. Communicative language teaching 30

CHAPTER TWO Language use 32

A Argument 32
B Discussion 50
    1. Idealization 50
    2. Itemization of skills 52
    3. Schemata 54
    4. Ambiguity 59
    5. Schematic anticipation 61
    6. Tautology and metaphor 62
    7. Perception 65
    8. Frame procedures 67
    9. Routine procedures 74
   10. Formulations 77
   11. Co-operative and territorial imperatives 78

CHAPTER THREE   Course design and methodology   80

A **Argument** 80
B **Discussion** 92
    1. Comprehension questions   92
    2. Procedural vocabulary   92
    3. Methodology   95
    4. Schematic types and genre   101
    5. Procedural types and cognitive style   102

CHAPTER FOUR   **In conclusion**   105

References   111

Index   119

Introduction

This book is an enquiry into the theoretical credentials of ESP — English for Specific Purposes — and, by implication, of LSP — language, any language, taught to the specification of purpose. The field is already a busy one, full of prospectors staking claims, working seams, with the usual crowd of attendant camp followers parasitic on their success. Why then add to the congestion?

Although there is a good deal of impressive industry in the field, it does not always seem to be directed by a clear understanding of the aims of the enterprise and the most effective means of achieving them. Vigorous digging is not an alternative to a knowledge of geology. On the whole, practical work on ESP has tended to proliferate without the benefit of theoretical reflection, and much of it is makeshift. Of those who do give serious thought to the principles underlying ESP practices, some argue that the practices are contingent modifications of general principles made by reference to administrative exigencies and the requirement of direct accountability, but not calling for any new conceptualization of language teaching pedagogy as such. Others take a contrary view, insisting that ESP calls for a reformulation of principles of approach; for special expertise in specific language description and in course preparation and teaching. But in the absence of any clear theoretical framework, it is very difficult to assess the cogency of the opposing arguments — difficult sometimes, indeed, to discern just what the arguments are. They, too, often have a somewhat makeshift appearance.

The purpose of this book is to provide such a framework. I offer it in no spirit of superior wisdom, but only in the hope that it might prove of some service for the clarification of current ideas and practices in this field. It is only a framework, a construct for convenience, and not a monument to truth.

I have, however, taken considerable care in its construction, and this is reflected in the way the book has been designed. This might at first sight appear somewhat eccentric, even perverse, and calls for some explanation. Chapters 1–3 each consist of two parts. Part A presents the essentials of the argument and Part B takes up issues arising from this argument which in my judgement warrant more detailed and documented discussion. These issues are marked by numbers in the text so as to indicate where reference to discussion points in Part B is to be made. The second part (B) of each chapter, therefore, is intended to provide a fuller exposition of the theory which gives warrant to the points made in the argument (Part A). The reason for this arrangement is that it seems to me that often the main lines of an argument can be distorted by the elaboration and the reference to other work which is necessary to place it in perspective. So I have presented them separately. This arrangement corresponds to the lecture + discussion format of spoken presentations, and allows me to indicate the depth of implication underlying issues in ESP without digression: I can step back to get these issues in proper perspective without losing sight of them. The intention is that the reader should read through Part A and then go on to Part B, referring back where necessary. S/he can, of course, choose to disregard Part B altogether, but that would be a pity, because the theoretical dimension of the argument would then diminish, with a consequent foreshortening of perspective. Chapter 4 recapitulates and concludes the argument of the preceding chapters.

In pursuing my argument, I have drawn a number of distinctions: aims/objectives; competence/capacity/; system/schema, and so on. This is a common practice of mine and has attracted some criticism. An apology would seem to be in order — but an apology more in the sense of a justification than an acknowledgement of offence. It should not be supposed that these distinctions express the belief that the universe is divided up into neat binary oppositions, that truth is reducible to a series of simple dualities. To suppose this is to mistake the nature and purpose of the kind of conceptual enquiry I am engaged on in this book. The distinctions I make are intended as devices of investigation, aids to understanding, and they are based on the principle of idealization upon which all systematic enquiry must depend. They do not represent reality, but act as points from which bearings on reality can be taken. So there is a distinction to be made — but enough. The point need, I hope, be laboured no further.

Nobody writes a book entirely on his own. The words that appear on the page have a long history of past discussions, of the unconscious adoption (and adaptation) of other ideas, of the influence of other minds. They emerge from what Henry James referred to as 'the deep well of unconscious cerebration'. A large number of students and colleagues have in this sense contributed to this book and they may share any praise there may be for its virtues, while avoiding any censure for its shortcomings.

The influence of one mind, however, calls for particular mention: that of my colleague C. J. Brumfit, who also took the trouble to make detailed comments on an earlier draft of the book. My specific and special thanks to him.

H. G. Widdowson
London December 1982

1 Learning purpose

A Argument

Over recent years, ESP has emerged as a particular sub-division of the general activity of teaching English to speakers of other languages. It has taken on all the appurtenances of a separate subject. People are appointed to teach it, courses have been devised to impart the special mystery of its methodology, journals have been founded to promote its advancement, and publishers have produced separate lists of their offerings in the field. It has become an institution. But what is so distinctive about it as to call for this institutional endowment of separate identity? Institutions, after all, develop from all kinds of causes, often from a convergence of random factors, and once established often remain because of the inertia of custom or the influence of self-interest long after the circumstances which created them have disappeared into history.

My intention in this essay is to enquire into the pedagogic justification for granting ESP its own particular claim in the general area of English teaching, to investigate the rational bases for its institutional existence. (B 1)*

Perhaps the first observation to make is that, in spite of the implied claim, an ESP course is in one sense really no more specific in its purposes than is one designed for general purpose English teaching (GPE for short). Syllabus designers and textbook writers have customarily worked to quite exact specifications, drawn up with reference to inventories of language items of one sort or another and directed at purposes represented by different stages of achievement, themselves defined by reference to some notion of eventual aims. In this respect, GPE is no less specific and purposeful than ESP. What distinguishes them is the way in which purpose is defined, and the manner of its implementation.

---

*Fuller discussion of issues indicated in this way will be found in the appropriately numbered section of Part B of each chapter.

In ESP, 'purpose' refers to the eventual practical use to which the language will be put in achieving occupational and academic aims. As generally understood, it is essentially, therefore, a *training* concept: having established as precisely as possible what learners need the language for, one then designs a course which converges on that need. The course is successful to the extent that it provides the learners with the restricted competence they need to meet their requirements. In GPE it is of course not possible to define purpose in this way. Instead it has to be conceived of in *educational* terms, as a formulation of objectives which will achieve a potential for later practical use. Here it is not a matter of developing a restricted competence to cope with a specified set of tasks, but of developing a general capacity for language use. Whereas, therefore, 'purpose' is a descriptive term in ESP, in GPE it is a theoretical term in that it has to be defined by reference to an educational belief about what provides most effectively for a future ability to use language. (**B** 2)

I am suggesting, then, that as generally conceived, ESP is essentially a training operation which seeks to provide learners with a restricted competence to enable them to cope with certain clearly defined tasks. These tasks constitute the specific purposes which the ESP course is designed to meet. The course, therefore, makes direct reference to eventual aims. GPE, on the other hand, is essentially an educational operation which seeks to provide learners with a general capacity to enable them to cope with undefined eventualities in the future. Here, since there are no definite aims which can determine course design, there has to be recourse to intervening objectives formulated by pedagogic theory. These objectives represent the potential for later realization and are, so to speak, the abstract projection of aims. In GPE, the actual use of language occasioned by communicative necessity is commonly a vague and distant prospect on the other side of formal assessment. It is crucial therefore that objectives should be formulated and assessed in such a way as to be a projection of eventual aims. With ESP, on the other hand, the prospect of actual language use is brought immediately into the foreground and into focus so that it serves both as the immediate objective and the eventual aim of learning. The distinction is summarized in tabular form on the opposite page.

I have in the preceding discussion made two distinctions which call for further comment. First, there is the distinction between aims and objectives. By objectives I mean the pedagogic intentions of a particular course of study to be achieved within the period of that course and in principle measurable by some assessment device at

ESP	specification of objectives: equivalent to aims	=	training: development of restricted competence
GPE	specification of objectives: leads to aims	=	education: development of general capacity

the end of the course. By aims I mean the purposes to which learning will be put *after* the end of the course. Thus a course may have as one of its objectives the development of the ability to carry out certain specific experiments in chemistry, but the aim of this exercise would refer to a more general capacity for problem solving and rational enquiry which learners could apply to later experience even if they had no further contact with chemistry for the rest of their lives. In English teaching, a course might specify objectives in terms of a set of lexical items or syntactic structures, or notions or functions, but its aims would be to develop an ability to exploit a knowledge of these elements in effective communication. (B 3)

A central problem in education is to know how to define objectives so that they project students towards the achievement of aims, how to fashion particular subjects so that they have relevance beyond themselves. A lack of motivation on the part of students may arise either from a rejection of the aims presupposed by the objectives, or from a rejection of the objectives as a valid mediation towards aims that they do accept. These two sources of student disaffection are not always distinguished, but they need to be, because they call for different remedies. If aims are rejected, you need to enquire into your concept of the nature of education. If objectives are rejected, you need to revise your pedagogy.

The second distinction I have made is between competence and capacity. The former term is a familiar one. In Chomsky's original formulation it refers to the speaker's knowledge of the sentences of his language and constitutes a generative device for the production and reception of correct linguistic forms. Over recent years the concept of competence has been extended to incorporate not only the speaker's knowledge of the language system, but his knowledge also of social rules which determine the appropriate use of linguistic forms. Thus communicative competence is said to include linguistic competence. But in both cases what is referred to is a conformity to pre-existing rules of behaviour as if instances of language use were only tokens of types of knowledge structure. What the concept of competence does not appear to account for is the ability to create meanings by exploiting the potential inherent in the language for continual modification in response to change. It is this ability that I refer to in using the term 'capacity'. Whereas 'competence' carries with it the implication that behaviour is determined by rule almost as if humans simply responded to linguistic and sociolinguistic control, 'capacity' carries with it the assumption that human beings are in control of their own destiny and exploit the rules at their disposal for their own ends. One might claim that both competence and capacity allow for creativity. But the creativity referred to in discussions of linguistic competence refers to the generative mechanism of grammar which allows for the production and reception of *sentences* never previously attested. The creativity associated with capacity refers to the ability to produce and understand *utterances* by using the resources of the grammar in association with features of context to make meaning, which is a function of the relationship between the two. Such utterances will not always be in direct correspondence with sentences at all and in this respect will not be always sanctioned by the system. (**B** 4)

With reference to these distinctions, we can define training as the development of competence to deal with a limited range of problems identified in advance. Courses of instruction are based on a specification of what these problems are and aim at providing trainees with formulae which can be applied to these problems. Obviously, some flexibility has to be allowed for, since there is always likely to be some lack of fit between formula and problem. But training can, of its nature, only allow for relatively minor adjustment. Difficulties will arise if a problem needs to be interpreted and redefined before it can fit a formula, or if a formula itself needs to be modified to account for an unforeseen problem. Such situations, which involve not simply the application but the exploitation of knowledge, call for the engagement of capacity. Increased flexibility to account for unpredictable eventualities shifts training towards education in that it sets up a division between objectives and aims, which would, in training, normally be conflated, and so seeks to develop capacity beyond the confines of limited competence.

So what I am saying is that increased specificity of language use means an increased restriction of competence and an assumption of similarity between formula and problem, and this allows for a conflation of the aims and objectives of instruction. The question that now arises is whether it is satisfactory to consider ESP as an exercise in training of this kind which circumvents issues in education.

ESP is not only divided off into an enclave within the wider boundaries of English teaching, it is also parcelled up into sub-divisions within itself. It is common, for example, to distinguish English for Occupational Purposes (EOP) from English for Academic Purposes (EAP). Each of these is then subject to further sub-division. Thus within EOP we might have English for Airline Pilots, for Waiters, for Secretaries, for Telephone Receptionists, and so on; and within EAP we might have English for different areas of academic study: physics, engineering, architecture, economics, and so on. And then we can go on to make further refinements, distinguishing, for example, between different types of secretary, or telephone receptionist, between different areas within academic disciplines, and so on. And so we might go on refining our distinctions along a scale of increasing specificity of purpose.

It is, however, difficult to see the point in this procedure. If purpose is interpreted simply as what people need to do with their language then there will of course be a whole host of different purposes associated with various universes of discourse, types of interaction and so on, and each will yield a different description. But the crucial issue is whether these differences have any implication for the principles of course design beyond the indication of content. Do they call for different concepts of learning? It is easy enough to say that people who need English for pursuing the occupation of a secretary will have different purposes from those who need it to pursue academic study. Obviously they will. But how do we define the *type* of purpose? What is the conceptual definition of such differences, as opposed to their purely descriptive differentiation? The problem about all the kinds of ESP that have been suggested is that they make up an observational list and have no status in theory.

In the absence of a theoretical basis for defining these differences within ESP, it is not surprising that most of the work in the field has been devoted to characterizing the particular features of each variety of use as separate universes of discourse. Two kinds of device have been developed to this end. One of them, register analysis, describes areas of use in terms of formal linguistic categories and aims at producing a specification of linguistic competence. The other, needs analysis, describes these areas in terms of communicative categories, notions, functions, and the skills required to give them linguistic realization, and aims at a specification of communicative competence. (**B** 5) In both cases, the analysis is reductionist and divisive: reductionist in the sense that language use is broken down into constituent atoms, and divisive in the sense that the operation aims at establishing what is most distinct about different varieties, rather than the common features which could lead us to identify them as variants of more general types. What these operations yield, then, is a profile for a particular area of language use, expressed, though, as a set of constituents. And in both cases the assumption is that this profile constitutes the specification for course design: that the descriptive units of the analysis can be used without modification as pedagogic units for teaching.

Although both of these devices draw on theory in their construction, neither of them is informed by a coherent theory of ESP. They are indeed operational instruments, rather than models, and they yield descriptions which have little explanatory value about the actual nature of communication in different circumstances of use. There is no indication of what the relationship between different branches of ESP might be, because there is no attempt to incorporate a theory of ESP in the model of description.

Instead of a theory we have an assumption that ESP is simply a matter of describing a particular area of language and then using this description as a course specification to impart to learners the necessary restricted competence to cope with this particular area. In other words, it is assumed that ESP is essentially a training exercise.

Now in some kinds of ESP, training, as I have defined it, may well be appropriate, since it services a restricted repertoire of behaviour where formulae and problems to be solved correspond quite closely. This would presumably be the case with the communication of air traffic control. (**B** 6) But it will obviously not do when the English taught is intended to be auxiliary to aims which are fundamentally educational. And here we can make a first move towards a comprehensive theoretical view of the field. We can suggest that the purposes in ESP are arranged along a scale of specificity with training at one end and education at the other. As one moves along the scale in the direction of education, one has to account increasingly for the development of capacity and, at the same time, one has to take into consideration the pedagogic problem of establishing objectives which are projections of final aims. At the training end of the scale, objectives and aims will converge into close correspondence and will seek to impart restricted competence. At the education end of the scale will cluster courses of English for academic purposes which require the development of communicative capacity and which will call for pedagogic decisions in the formulation of objectives. At this end of the scale, ESP shades into GPE.

One or two observations must be made about the view of ESP that I am proposing here. First, although certain occupational courses might be located at the training end of the spectrum, the most specific end, this does not mean that learners will derive from them no educational benefit and will be deprived of the chance to develop communicative capacity. The purpose of a course may be to impart a quite restricted competence in the interests of cost effectiveness in the use of human resources to achieve certain results. If the learner can, at the end of the course, exchange the necessary information from the control tower, follow instructions in a repair manual, and so on, then the course will have achieved its training objective. But the trainee, in acquiring this required competence, may well have developed at the same time a potential for later exploitation in other areas of activity. The learner may always go beyond the goals of the course of instruction, just as he or she may always fall short of them. So when I refer to training, I am referring to the purpose of the instruction, not to its total effect on the trainee.

A second point to be made, related to the first, has to do with the relationship between competence and capacity. As I mentioned earlier, I define capacity as the ability to exploit a knowledge of the conventions of a language and its use for the creation of linguistic behaviour which does not conform to type. But capacity in this sense depends upon, even if it is not determined by, a knowledge of the rules, even if this knowledge is in certain respects incomplete or imperfect; so capacity presupposes a point of reference in competence. I shall be taking this matter up again in greater detail in the next chapter, when I shall argue that the whole discourse process of meaning negotiation can be referred to this relationship between competence and capacity. For the moment, the point to make is that since language use cannot (except in certain unusual circumstances) be entirely a matter of conformity, nor entirely a matter of unconstrained freedom from convention, language education will always have a training aspect, and language training always contain some aspects of education. The problem for any ESP course design is to find its place on the continuum.

A final point that I ought to mention now has to do with the relationship between the objectives of a course and the methodology which is used in fulfilling them. So far, discussion has centred on how the objectives of ESP might be defined in respect of terminal aims. I have, however, suggested that the common assumption that a specification of such aims should determine course design is open to question. What is also open to question is the extent to which the approach to teaching used to implement this design is, or should be, independent of such aims. How far, then, do decisions about the objectives of a course carry implications about its design and the methodology used to teach it? These questions are the central concern of Chapter 3.

Meanwhile, it will be useful to summarize the points I have made in this present chapter.

All language courses are designed to a specification and in this sense can all be said to be directed at specific purposes. In general language teaching, however, where the eventual use of the language being learned is not clearly discernible, purposes are specified by objectives, pedagogic constructs which seek to provide for the achievement of practical communicative aims when occasion arises after the completion of the course. Thus in the familiar structural syllabus, the eventual communicative aim of language learning was freely acknowledged and the assumption was that a definition of objectives in terms of sentence construction would provide for the reaching of the aim. The recent shift of emphasis from structure to notion and function, from formal to communicative categories, does not alter the aim but leads to a reconsideration of the objectives in achieving it. (B 7) Whereas purpose is understood as a matter of objective in general purpose English (GPE) often given formal recognition by a public examination, purpose in ESP is understood as a matter of aim. That is to say, since the actual practical needs for the language can be described in advance, they can represent a quite precise specification for the course. When a course is designed to meet aims directly, then there is no need to set up an intervening stage of pedagogically defined objectives. This would appear to be the case with ESP, as commonly conceived: it would seem that its aim-oriented character allows its practitioners to conflate objectives and aims and so avoid some of the most troublesome problems of pedagogy.

This conflation of objectives and aims has the effect of character-izing ESP as an area of training rather than education, thereby giving it an appealing cost-effective appearance. However, there are certain difficulties about this reduction of pedagogic complexity. It presupposes, to begin with, that it is possible and desirable to restrict the learner to the acquisition of a particular repertoire of formulae which can be applied directly to the solution of a predictable range of problems; that is to say, that the learner's purposes can be met by his being provided with a restricted competence. An increasing specificity of purpose will lead to an increasing confinement of competence as the formulae to be learned and the problems they are to be applied to come closer into correspondence. But the situations of language use which simply call for the automatic application of formulae and the submissive conformity to established rules are relatively rare. There are occupations (airline pilots and seafarers) and occasions in more general language use (polite greeting formulae, for example) which call for little more than the running through of a routine; but generally speaking, effective language use requires the creative exploitation of the meaning potential inherent in language rules — requires, in other words, what I have called communicative capacity. It is this ability which enables the language user to negotiate the gap between formula and the problem and which has to be provided for in the formulation of pedagogic objectives.

This being so, the purposes of ESP courses will not be adequately accounted for if they are so specifically defined as to confine the learners to a range of stock responses constituting a restricted competence, leaving no room for the development of capacity. Such courses would in effect be little more than phrase books, taught as patterns of conditioned response, as automatic formula–problem correlations.

I have suggested that in the field of ESP, courses and materials have often been devised without taking into account the issues I have raised in this chapter, and in consequence it has become a busy area of basically *ad hoc* operational activity without reference to any clear theoretical principles. I have tried to indicate that to set about establishing such principles, one has to recognize that aim-oriented and objective-oriented purposes are different and that their relationship poses complex pedagogic problems, that the concept of specificity carries implications about the nature of language ability which I have tried to clarify with the competence/capacity distinction. I now want to consider these problems and implications more closely.

B   Discussion

1.   *Historical perspectives*

The recognition of the importance of relating the teaching of
language to the particular needs of students is not as recent as might
be supposed by the aura of revelation which surrounds some
writing on ESP. As early as 1921, H. E. Palmer makes the crucial, if
obvious point:

> We cannot design a language course until we know something
> about the students for whom the course is intended, for a
> programme of study depends on the aim or aims of the students.
> (Palmer 1964: 129)

Palmer gives the following examples of particular aims:

> The clerk or merchant will specialize in the commercial language
> and learn how to draw up bills of lading or to conduct business
> correspondence. The hotel-keeper or waiter will concentrate on
> hotel colloquial, as also will the tourist or tripper. The *littérateur*
> will aim straight at the literature and disdain any of the non-
> aesthetic aspects or branches. Every calling or profession will
> seek its own particular line, and for each there will be a particular
> aim. (Palmer 1964: 25)

Palmer also mentions (1964: 24) the selective concentration on
particular language skills or abilities, as does Morris, thirty-five
years on:

> In the case of private pupils or of a special course where the
> language is required for a known purpose, e.g. a proposed visit to
> an English-speaking country, access to specialized reading, com-
> mercial correspondence, or translation into the vernacular, all
> activities not contributory to the promotion of the particular
> ability are presumably superfluous. Although all language fea-
> tures are not unconnected, it is possible to concentrate on one or
> several of them almost exclusively. Much time and energy would
> therefore be saved if both aims and methods were subordinated
> to the special purpose. (Morris 1954: 20)

On the face of it, there seems to be no essential difference of view
between what is said in these quotations from Palmer and Morris
and the definition of ESP proposed by Strevens, twenty-five years
on:

The following is offered as a working definition of ESP: 'ESP entails the provision of English language instruction:

(i) devised to meet the learner's particular needs;
(ii) related in themes and topics to designated occupations or areas of study;
(iii) selective (i.e. 'not general') as to language content;
(iv) when indicated, restricted as to the language 'skills' included'. (Strevens 1980: 108–9)

There is a difference of perspective between these writers, however. Palmer and Morris accommodate specificity of purpose within the general principles of language teaching pedagogy, so that it calls for no separate definition. By 1980, ESP is established as an institutional reality and so needs a definition to give recognition to its status. Once it is established and recognized as a separate area of activity, the assumption naturally arises that it must be based on *different* principles from those of language teaching pedagogy in general. What these principles are thought to be is indicated in another definition:

> ... we may say that an ESP course is purposeful and is aimed at the successful performance of occupational or educational roles. It is based on a rigorous analysis of students' needs and should be 'tailor-made'. (Robinson 1980: 13)

The first part of this quotation is entirely consistent with the views expressed by Palmer and Morris. The second implies that student need is a determining factor in course design and overrides other considerations. Such a view would not have found favour with Palmer:

> Our programme should be something other than a rigid procedure based on any one particular principle, however logical that principle may seem to be. There are many logical principles, and we must strive to incorporate all of them into whatever programme we design. (Palmer 1964: 28)

I shall be arguing in this book (as I have argued elsewhere, e.g. Widdowson 1981a, 1981b) that work on ESP has suffered through too rigid an adherence to the principle of specificity of eventual purpose as a determining criterion for course design. This has arisen, I suggest, because ESP has been removed from the context of language teaching pedagogy in general, where Morris and Palmer place it.

The point, then, in referring to these earlier writers is not just to play the familiar game of finding historical precedence for apparent innovation, but to indicate what seems to me to be a significant difference of attitude. Morris and Palmer acknowledge the importance of making provision for specific needs *within the framework of language teaching pedagogy in general*. The assumption of separate and special status, with the acronym ESP as the blazon, is a later development, beginning, I would think, in the early 1960s.

The reasons for the development cannot easily be traced in the usual murk of history, but they have something to do with the changing pattern of requirements for English in the emerging Third World (for brief comments on this, see Widdowson 1968: Chapter 4, Halliday, McIntosh, and Strevens 1964: 189–90) and the coincident interest in language registers arising mainly out of the work of Halliday and his associates in Edinburgh (see e.g. Halliday, McIntosh, and Strevens 1964: 87–94). There was thus at this time a coincidence of two different kinds of movement. One created socio-economic changes which needed to be serviced by English language resources. The other seemed to provide a mode of linguistic description which rendered the language particularly serviceable. ESP was generally seen as the natural pedagogic issue of this circumstantial coupling. It is important, however, to distinguish ESP as a socio-economic phenomenon with its attendant administrative consequences from the notion of linguistic and pedagogic specificity. Failure to make this distinction has caused a good deal of confusion. Whether and to what extent the two can or must be related has to be demonstrated and cannot be simply presupposed.

An excellent documentation of the development of ESP over the past two decades or so is provided in Swales 1983, which is a selection of papers by various hands arranged in chronological sequence with perceptive comments by Swales himself, pointing to the historical significance of each paper.

For a detailed exposition of the historical provenance of language teaching pedagogy in general, which indicates that ESP can be traced far further into the past than 1921, see Howatt 1984.

2.   *Education and training*

The distinction I draw here between education and training is a recurring theme in the writing of R. S. Peters. Consider the following quotations:

The concept of 'training' has application when (i) there is some specifiable type of performance that has to be mastered, (ii) practice is required for a mastery of it, (iii) little emphasis is placed on the underlying rationale. (Peters 1967: 13)

... a person could be a trained ballet-dancer or have mastered an eminently worthwhile skill, such as pottery-making, without being educated. What might be lacking is something to do with knowledge and understanding; for being educated demands more than being highly skilled. An educated man must also possess some body of knowledge and some kind of conceptual scheme to raise this above the level of a collection of disjointed facts. This implies some understanding of principles for the organization of facts. (Peters 1973a: 18)

However, it would appear that Peters's formulation of the distinction as related to education in general does not fit the particular case of language teaching that I am concerned with. For in GPE, or ESP language teaching for speakers of other languages, we *are* concerned with skills in the Peters sense, that is to say, with the practical deployment of principles, and not with the knowledge and understanding of these principles as such. In respect of language teaching, therefore, I would wish to say that an educational approach is one which develops an understanding of principles *in order to extend the range of their application*. A person educated in a certain language, as opposed to one who is trained only in its use for a restricted set of predictable situations, is someone who is able to relate what he or she knows to circumstances other than those which attended the acquisition of that knowledge. To put it another way, education in a language presupposes the internalization of what Halliday calls 'meaning potential'. It is the ability to realize this potential that I refer to as capacity (see Discussion 4 in this chapter).

It might clarify matters if, at this point, I associated education and training with the distinction I have made elsewhere (Widdowson 1978) between skills and abilities. The purpose of training is to impart a set of skills, which are, in effect, a repertoire of responses tagged with appropriate stimulus indicators, a set of paired associations. A *linguistic* skill involves the linking of an abstract linguistic rule with its concrete expression: the relating of form and substance. Although I did not previously conceive of the possibility, one can think of a *communicative* skill as involving a repertoire of linguistic forms tagged with appropriate situational or notional/

functional indicators: the relating of form and situation. Whereas, then, one might reasonably think of training as the imparting of *skills*, education is essentially a matter of developing *abilities*, understood as cognitive constructs which allow for the individual's adjustment to changing circumstances. Thus abilities provide for further learning through creative endeavour: what is given can be altered by what is new. Skills, on the other hand, confine the possessor to conformity: what is new cannot be accommodated into given categories.

It would seem to follow from this that skills can be directly imparted by instruction, whereas abilities cannot. This would seem to accord with Peters's view of the educational process:

> The typical term for the educational process by means of which people are brought to understand principles is 'teaching'; for 'teach', unlike 'train' or 'instruct', suggests that a *rationale* is to be grasped behind the skill or body of knowledge. (Peters 1967: 19)

It is important to note, however, that teaching stimulates the educational process only by indirect effect which, it seems to me, must be mediated by learning. In the training of skills, the operation fails if the output behaviour of those being trained does not match the input instruction. Trainer and trainee are converse terms, as their morphology implies. There is no such reflexivity in education: teaching and learning are not converse activities in the same sense. Learners are not teachees (see Widdowson 1981a). People 'are brought to understand principles' and, I would add, to an ability to act upon them, by means of *learning*, which teaching serves only to facilitate. If this is not so, then teaching in effect becomes training, and when it is directed at rationale rather than practical skill, it takes the form of indoctrination. Ryle indicates the importance of recognizing the non-converseness of teaching and learning in the following way:

> We started off with the apparent paradox that though the teacher in teaching is doing something to his pupil, yet the pupil has learned virtually nothing unless he becomes able and ready to do things of his own motion other than what the teacher exported to him. We asked: 'How in logic can the teacher dragoon his pupil into thinking for himself, impose initiative upon him, drive him into self-motion, conscript him into volunteering, enforce originality upon him, or make him operate spontaneously? The answer is that we cannot — and the reason why we half-felt that

he must do so was that we were unwittingly enslaved by the crude, semi-hydraulic idea that in essence to teach is to pump propositions like 'Waterloo, 1815' into the pupils' ears, until they regurgitate them automatically. (Ryle 1967: 118)

What Ryle refers to as 'hydraulic injection' has its justification, however, in a straightforward training context, where the purpose is to shape behaviour to a prescribed pattern. Here, people are *given* training or instruction and they succeed to the extent that they *receive* it. As Ryle indicates, teaching is not given and received in this way: it has to be transmuted into learning before it can be effective.

I would wish to suggest, then, that the difference between training and education (at least as far as language teaching is concerned) is not, as Peters claims, that the latter provides a rationale whereas the former does not, but rather that training seeks to impose a *conformity* to certain established patterns of knowledge and behaviour, usually in order to carry out a set of clearly defined tasks, where the problem is recognizably a token of a formula type. Education, however, seeks to provide for *creativity* whereby what is learned is a set of schemata and procedures for adapting them to cope with problems which do not have a ready-made formulaic solution. In this sense we may say that training tends to convergence and a reliance on established technique, whereas education tends towards divergence and a readiness to break from the confinement of prescribed practices (see Hudson 1967).

If the divergent tendency is followed through to its logical conclusion, education becomes a process of self-realization untrammelled by purpose defined by institutional requirement. In effect, it becomes 'deschooled' (see Illich 1970). Whereas extreme convergence would pay exclusive attention to the established needs of society and establish aims without regard to objectives ('pure' training), extreme divergence would be exclusively concerned with the needs of the individual and focus on objectives without regard to aims ('pure' education).

The methodology for convergence would naturally be teacher-centred, that for divergence learner-centred. See Discussion 3 below.

It should be noted that the distinction I have drawn here between education and training is a conceptual one, intended as a device for clarifying what seem to me to be important differences in pedagogic principle. This device can be thought of as a scale, with training at one end and education at the other. Naturally, in practice different courses of instruction will be positioned somewhere between the two extremes. Thus a course with a primary training purpose will generally need to allow for a measure of adaptability and so have an educational element, and a course with a primary educational purpose will generally need to make provision for techniques associated with training. But the fact that there is no absolute category division between courses of education and training does not, of course, invalidate the distinction in principle; nor does it undermine its relevance to our understanding of how the principle works out in practice.

3. *Aims, objectives, and learner needs*

The absence of distinction between aims and objectives leads to an ambiguity in the expression 'learner needs'. On the one hand, it can refer to what the learner has to do with the language once he has learned it: in this sense it has to do with aims. On the other hand, it can refer to what the learner has to do *in order to learn*: in this sense, it relates to pedagogic objectives. I discuss this ambiguity in more detail in Widdowson 1981b.

There may be a case for concentrating on the learner's needs in the first sense in order to delimit initially the language to be included in a course; but needs of the second kind — learning needs — will have to be taken into account in the methodological implementation of course proposals. It is interesting to note how the two kinds of need were related in the design of structural syllabuses of the conventional kind. Specification of content was derived basically from a frequency count of items in a representative corpus of language, supplemented by criteria of range and coverage. This was intended to account for the language that the learner would be most likely to encounter and so was aim-oriented. But the specification was then modified to include items which were likely to facilitate learning, quite apart from their relevance to aims. This modification was pedagogically motivated and objective-oriented. For further discussion, see Mackey 1965: Chapter 6, Widdowson 1968: Chapter 2.

Needs analysis for ESP has generally been concerned with the specification of aims in this sense, and methodological modification has not been very much in evidence. This is not· to say that the importance of such modification has not been recognized. Munby, for example, mentions it as a constraint (among others) on the implementation of the aim specification derived from his 'operational instrument':

> These implementational constraints are, of course, significant in the modification of syllabus specifications and production of materials, but that is the next stage in course design and should not take place until after the output from the operational instrument has been obtained. (Munby 1978: 217)

In practice in ESP, however, learning needs as defined by pedagogic objectives have generally been demoted in favour of learner needs as defined by eventual aims. The second order priority that Munby gives them naturally shifts them from the centrality they ought to have in the educational process.

This is not to say that aims should not be defined as a preliminary step towards the main business of establishing objectives: indeed, it would be a sound methodological procedure to do so. The problem is that in ESP they often seem to be the exclusive preoccupation of course designers, so that objectives are relegated to a peripheral status. This is one consequence of shifting ESP out of the context of general language teaching pedagogy (see Discussion 1 in this chapter).

My use of this pair of terms is, I think, consistent with Bloom's notion of educational objectives (Bloom 1956/72), as is evident from the way the purpose of his taxonomy is described:

> ... this taxonomy is designed to be a classification of student behaviours which represent the intended outcome of the educational process ... What we are classifying is the intended behaviour of students — the ways in which individuals are to act, think, or feel as the result of participating in some unit of instruction. By educational objectives, we mean explicit formulations of the ways in which students are expected to be changed by the educative (sic) process. (Bloom 1972: 12, 26)

These formulations draw on a range of different considerations:

> One type of source commonly used in thinking about objectives is the information available about the students. What is their present level of development? What are their needs? What are their interests? Another source for objectives is available from investigations of the conditions and problems of contemporary life which make demands on young people and adults and which provide opportunities for them. What are the activities that

individuals are expected to perform? What are the problems they are likely to encounter? What are the opportunities they are likely to have for service and self-realization?

Another source of suggestions for objectives comes from the nature of the subject matter ... What is the conception of the subject field? What are the types of learning which can arise from a study of that subject matter? What are the contributions that the subject can make in relation to other subjects? ... educational objectives must be related to a psychology of learning. The faculty must distinguish goals that are feasible from goals which are unlikely to be attained in the time available, under the conditions which are possible, and with the group of students to be involved. (Bloom 1972: 26, 27)

One may contrast this catalogue of questions to be taken into account in defining educational objectives with the stark definitions of ESP aims based only on the one consideration of student needs, understood as his or her eventual practical requirements.

It is of interest to note that many of the factors mentioned by Bloom are taken into account in the approach to needs analysis developed by Richterich for the Council of Europe Modern Languages Project (see Richterich 1973). This approach (as is pointed out in Trim 1980) has increasingly recognized the crucial relevance of learner variables and the inadequacy of a specification which simply identifies objectives in respect of eventual target behaviour. As Trim puts it:

In this perspective, 'needs analysis' comes to mean the whole cluster of techniques which lead to an understanding of the parameters of the learning situations: ego, fellow learners, teacher(s), administrators, course-writers, producers, social agencies, career expectations and job satisfaction, social dynamics, learner-type and resource analysis, etc, are relevant factors in addition to the original predicated communicative behaviour. Since none of these are constant, analysis becomes a central aspect of course management and a most important aspect of the long climb to that self-reliance and autonomy which, we hope, eventually allow the learner to take charge of his own learning. (Trim 1980: 63)

To define needs in this way means, as Trim suggests, that they cannot be fixed in advance but must be a matter of negotiation as part of the actual educational process. This involves shifting the centre of attention from the teacher to the learner as the agent of change, and from the requirements of groups defined by their occupational and academic roles (secretaries, engineers, physicists) to the claims of individual experience and the development of self-knowledge. If this shift goes too far, of course, one arrives at 'pure' education (as referred to in the preceding Discussion) and its associated permissive pedagogy of non-intervention (see Allwright 1977, 1979, Holec 1980).

4.   *Competence and capacity*

It might be objected that all I am doing here is indulging in terminological chicanery by using a new term 'capacity' instead of the well-established one 'communicative competence'. But this latter term carries with it two related implications which I want the concept of capacity to keep clear of. Firstly, it refers to an *analyst's* construct and not a *user's*: it is not, in ethnomethodological parlance, a member category (cf. Sacks 1979). That is to say, competence, whether linguistic or communicative, refers to those aspects of human language behaviour that can be formalized in a model of description. In Chomsky's original formulation, for example, competence is defined as a knowledge of sentences possessed by an ideal speaker/listener in a homogeneous speech community (Chomsky 1965: 3). Such an idealization is necessary to bring language data within the scope of systematic analysis as determined by a particular theoretical perspective. It does not follow at all that this analysis corresponds to any reality in the minds of the language users themselves. The grammarian sets up his model of language on the basis of a set of cultural beliefs which he does not necessarily share with the people whose behaviour he is analysing. In this respect he is no different from the anthropologist or sociologist, and he runs the same risk of ethnocentrism. There is, then, no necessary coincidence of analyst and user models of language. Competence refers to what the grammarian for methodological reasons *represents* as language knowledge: it does not refer to the language user's mode of knowing. (For further discussion, see Widdowson 1979 Chapter 18; 1980.)

The objections to Chomsky's concept of competence, as expressed by Hymes in particular, are directed not at its analytic character, but at its inadequacy in not accounting for other aspects of language knowledge apart from the knowledge of sentence structure. Thus in Hymes's model of communicative competence the analytic perspective is retained: it is not a model of member knowledge of language use, but one which provides the means for analysing member behaviour from outside. This is how Hymes describes it:

> If an adequate theory of language users and language use is to be developed, it seems that judgments must be recognized to be in fact not of two kinds but of four. [The two kinds referred to here are 'grammaticality, with respect to competence', and 'acceptability, with respect to performance'.] And if linguistic theory is to be integrated with theory of communication and culture, this fourfold distinction must be stated in a sufficiently generalized way. I would suggest, then, that for language and for other forms of communication (culture), four questions arise:
>
> 1 whether (and to what degree) something is formally *possible*;
> 2 whether (and to what degree) something is *feasible* in virtue of the means of implementation available;
> 3 whether (and to what degree) something is *appropriate* (adequate, happy, successful) in relation to a context in which it is used and evaluated;
> 4 whether (and to what degree) something is in fact done, actually *performed*, and what its doing entails.
>
> ... These questions may be asked from the standpoint of a system *per se*, or from the standpoint of persons. An interest in competence dictates the latter standpoint here ... There is an important sense in which a normal member of a community has knowledge with respect to all these aspects of the communicative systems available to him. He will interpret or assess the conduct of others and himself in ways that reflect a knowledge of each (possible, feasible, appropriate), done (if so, how often). There is an important sense in which he would be said to have a capability with regard to each. (Hymes 1972: 281–2)

It is clear that what Hymes has in mind here is a person's ability to make judgements about the extent to which a linguistic expression conforms to pre-existing norms for language activity, whether this be cognitive or communicative. It is this capability for assessment that constitutes communicative competence. But such a capability is *analytic* and is directed at recognizing not the meaning that an expression *communicates*, but the degree of normality that it *indicates*. The focus of attention is on what the expression signals *other than intended meaning*. In this respect, communicative competence, or capability, is similar in kind to the ability to carry

out a stylistic analysis in the manner of Crystal and Davy, which
also involves asking questions:

> Putting it crudely, the general question to be asking is, 'Apart
> from the message being communicated, what other kind of
> information does the utterance give us?'
> (Crystal and Davy 1969: 81)

Hymes' capability is, then, essentially ethnographic. Capacity, in
the sense I intend, is essentially ethnomethodological. That is to
say, it is the ability to use a knowledge of language as a resource for
the creation of meaning, and is concerned not with assessment but
interpretation. Now it is true that Hymes does mention 'interpret'
as well as 'assess', but all four of his main 'parameters' relate to the
latter, not the former, except that he adds to the last, almost as if it
were an afterthought, the phrase: 'and what its doing entails'. But if
we are to define communicative competence as ability for use, what
'something' entails is a crucial question which applies to *all* of the
parameters mentioned. Consider, for example, this piece of language:

> Underwater eyes, an eel's
> Oil of water body, neither fish nor beast is the otter . . .
> (Ted Hughes)

We may be able to assess the relative possibility and feasibility of
this expression, note that it is abnormal in a number of ways, but
still fail to discover what it entails, what interpretation is to be
placed on it. Such an assessment would seem to be evidence for
Hymes of communicative competence. What I am concerned with
is not this analytic capability, but the interpretative capacity which
enables the user to make sense of expressions of varying possibility,
feasibility, and so on.

So one reason for preferring the term 'capacity' to 'communicative competence' is that the latter seems to imply an analytic, rather
than a user, perspective and to assume an equation between user
and analyst models of language. The second reason, also touched
on in the foregoing discussion, is that competence seems to imply
conformity, either to code (linguistic competence) or to social
convention (communicative competence). The assumption seems to
be made that language behaviour is rule governed, determined by a
knowledge system which has only to be invoked and applied on
particular occasions for communication to take place. In other
words, language behaviour is a matter of compliance. But by

'capacity' I mean the ability to exploit the resources for meaning in a language which have only partially been codified as competence and are only partially describable, therefore, in grammars. Capacity is, therefore, as implied previously in this chapter, the natural language analogue of the educational process. It cannot be imparted by training and cannot be accounted for in models of grammar. As Lyons observes:

> To attempt to build into the linguist's model of the language-system all the factors which determine our capacity to interpret utterances would be to nullify the very concept of a language-system. (Lyons 1977: 420)

Just so. It is the linguist's task to set up models for the representation of linguistic competence, the knowledge of what has been codified as system. Such models do not account for the user's capacity for the creative exploitation of knowledge for the making of meaning. However, they must *presuppose* capacity, since it is this which activates the acquisition of competence in the first place. Chomsky speaks of the innate 'predisposition' or 'language-forming capacity' of the child. This capacity is identified with a language acquisition device (LAD) which enables it to learn the sentences of, that is to say to acquire a competence in, a particular language (Chomsky 1965: 29–30). My point is quite simply that this capacity is not used up by conversion into competence, as sometimes seems to be suggested, but remains as an active force for continuing creativity. If this were not so, there would be no way of explaining how language users are able to produce and interpret innovative expressions which do not conform to established rules and which are, therefore, beyond the scope of their competence. There would be no way, either, of accounting for features of a second language learner's interlanguage which cannot be characterized as transfer from the first language. Such features lead Corder to propose the hypothesis that:

> ... some at least of the strategies adopted by the learner of a second language are substantially the same as those by which a first language is acquired. (Corder 1967: 164–5)

The existence of such strategies presupposes the continuity of capacity beyond the formation of one or more competence. It is interesting to note that Palmer, thirty-five years before Chomsky's *Syntactic Structures*, talks about 'natural or spontaneous capacities for acquiring speech' and observes:

These capacities are not limited to the acquiring of our mother tongue, but are also available for one or more languages in addition. The young child possesses these capacities in the active state; consequently he picks up a second or third language in the same manner as he does the first. The adult possesses these same capacities, but generally in a latent state; by disuse he has allowed them to lapse. (Palmer 1964: 127)

My argument would be that capacity never falls into disuse, but continues as a force for the realization of what Halliday calls the 'meaning potential' of language. Its operation in the acquisition of second language systems, as discussed, for example, in Richards 1974, Hatch 1978, Corder 1981, is evidence of its more general function of creating meaning in use from the resources available, whether these are actually codified in established systems or not. So it is that we can discern a resemblance between expressions associated with the inter-languages of learners and those which appear in the work of creative writers. We call the former *error* — evidence of *deficiency* — whereas we call the latter *verbal art* — evidence of *proficiency*, and of a particularly high order. This should not prevent us from recognizing that they derive essentially from the same creative source. Both reveal the workings of capacity. This being so, the suppression of 'error' by the imposition of correctness will also tend to suppress the very force that activates the learning process itself. It is considerations like these (though not made explicit in these terms) that lend support to those who argue for the priority of fluency over accuracy (see, for example, Brumfit 1979, 1981).

The concept of capacity has, I think, a direct bearing on Krashen's monitor theory of language acquisition and learning (Krashen 1981, 1982). It seems to me that acquisition in the Krashen sense is essentially the operation of capacity, and what he refers to as learning is the acceptance of norms of correctness associated with competence in a particular language. Abnormalities occur when for a variety of reasons these norms are not in force: either because they are not known, or because the creative demands of communication or self-expression prevent their engagement. I see no need to postulate the existence of two separate systems. It seems to me that what we have is a developmental process which yields different stages of approximation to accepted norms and which is a function of the relationship between the acquiring capacity and the social constraints of an established competence.

Nor do I see any reason why this capacity should not operate on data which are consciously learned — quite apart from the problem of knowing whether they are consciously learned or not.

5. *Register analysis and needs analysis*

I am using the terms 'register analysis' and 'needs analysis' in the sense in which they are commonly understood. The former has been defined quite explicitly as being a characterization of texts in respect of their formal linguistic properties:

> Registers ... differ primarily in form ... the crucial criteria of any given register are to be found in its grammar and its lexis ... It is by their formal properties that registers are defined. If two samples of language activity from what, on non-linguistic grounds, could be considered different situation-types show no differences in grammar or lexis, they are assigned to one and the same register ... (Halliday, McIntosh and Strevens 1964: 88–9)

An early demonstration of register analysis in this sense appears in Huddleston *et al.* 1968, a later one in Lee Kok Cheong 1978. Its application in the delimitation of ESP course content is exemplified in Ewer and Latorre 1969, and discussed in Ewer and Latorre 1967, and Ewer and Hughes-Davies 1971.

The point about register analysis, defined and applied in this way, is that it is an operation on *text* and does not, as such, reveal how language is used in the discourse process. One can, of course, draw informal conclusions about this by speculating on the significance of the analysis, but it does not emerge as a function of the analysis itself, quite simply because linguistic forms do not reliably signal their pragmatic value in particular contexts of use. I have dwelt on this point elsewhere (Widdowson 1979 Chapters 2 and 3) (and shall refer to it again in the next chapter), but some still find it elusive (see, for example, Ewer and Boys 1981, which I discuss in more detail in Chapter 3).

There is no reason in principle why registers, or varieties, or rhetorical types should not be characterized by reference to the communicative properties of linguistic forms in context. Work along such lines has been carried out (e.g. Lackstrom, Selinker and Trimble 1973, Swales 1981b, Tarone *et al.* 1981 — which I refer to in the following chapter). But it is not register analysis in the conventional sense.

In the same way, needs analysis can be carried out as a

straightforward register analysis, itemizing the occurrence of formal linguistic features. Indeed, this is precisely what is done in the work of Ewer and Latorre. But I am using 'needs analysis' here to refer to an approach which characterizes language behaviour in terms of the notions and functions described in Van Ek 1975 and Wilkins 1976 and which has its most exhaustive exemplification in Munby 1978. I shall be referring to this work in Chapter 3.

6. Restricted languages

The language of air traffic control is 'restricted' in the sense that it occurs in a specifiable set of what Firth calls 'limited situational contexts'.

When I was consulted by the Air Ministry on the outbreak of war with Japan, I welcomed the opportunity of service in the Royal Air Force because I saw at once that the operating of reconnaissance and fighter aircraft by the Japanese could be studied by applying the concept of the limited situational contexts of war, the operative language of which we needed to know urgently and quickly. We were not going to meet the Japanese socially, but only in such contexts of fighting as required some form of spoken Japanese. A kind of operational linguistics was the outcome.... (Firth 1957: 182)

See also Palmer 1968: 112.

There is, however, a difference between the language of air traffic control and that of Japanese fighter pilots. The former is a *prescribed* code, a closed system of conventionally accepted verbal routines devised for the purpose and subscribed to by international agreement. The latter is a *described* set of common occurrences: it is an account of what pilots actually say when they carry out their various flying activities.

It is obviously easier to provide training in a use of language that is prescribed, rather than described. In the latter case, no matter how limited the contexts, there is always the chance that a situation may occur which has not been accounted for in the description, where a problem arises for which there is no formula. This, in principle, cannot happen with prescription. It is because of the possibility, in described language use, of a gap between formula and problem, that even the most exact training must have some educational element, why there must always be some provision for the development of capacity.

7. *Communicative language teaching*

Generally speaking, this shift of emphasis has had the effect of identifying objectives more closely with aims. One result of this is the widespread (and I believe mistaken) belief that if language is to be taught *for* communication it has necessarily to be presented *as* communication, that every classroom activity must bear the hall-mark of 'authenticity'. No doubt the title of my own book (Widdowson 1978) has made its own contribution to this misconception, and I wish now that I had chosen the more accurate and less misleading title 'Teaching language *for* communication'.

Authenticity (like needs) is a term which creates confusion because of a basic ambiguity. It can, on the one hand, be used to refer to actually attested language produced by native speakers for a normal communicative purpose. In this sense it refers to naturalistic textual data. But the term can also be used, quite legitimately, to refer to the communicative activity of the language user, to the engagement of interpretative procedures for making sense, even if these procedures are operating on and with textual data which are not authentic in the first sense. An authentic stimulus in the form of attested instances of language does not guarantee an authentic response in the form of appropriate language activity. It was in order to remove this ambiguity that I suggested (Widdowson 1979, Chapter 12) that we should retain the term 'authenticity' to refer to activity (i.e. process) and use the term 'genuine' to refer to attested instances of language (i.e. product).

But even if one interprets '*as* communication' as having to do with authentic activity in this sense, it is still open to question whether this can or should always be given first priority in the classroom. There are, after all, certain skills of an automatic habitual kind which are presupposed in the ability to communicate but which do not generally have a directly executive function in language use. They are, as it were, the backstage facilitators which have to be forgotten while the play is in progress. In natural language use, lower level skills are pushed down into automatic dependency on higher level abilities. The discrimination of sounds or orthographic shapes, for example, is normally carried out below the level of conscious awareness, thereby leaving the mind free to engage with higher things. Such skills have to be learned in order to be disregarded, since to be aware of their operation would be to disrupt normal communicative behaviour. Although they cannot, therefore, figure explicitly in the presentation of language *as* communication, they have a crucial role to play in the learning of language *for* communication.

The problem in language teaching here corresponds to the general educational problem referred to earlier in this chapter: how can objectives (learning language for communication) be defined so that they account for eventual aims (using language as communication)? To put it another way: how can we use contrived means to achieve a natural end?

2 Language use

A Argument

In the preceding chapter, I made a distinction between competence and capacity and pointed out that increased specificity of objectives will tend to concentrate on the former at the expense of the latter. I suggested that the consequence of this would be to diminish the learner's ability to cope with natural language use. The question now arises as to how one might be specific about the objectives of a course so that they might be directed towards a particular set of aims without compromising the necessary educational achievement of capacity. In other words, what kind of specification is necessary to design effective courses of ESP at different points on the scale of specificity?

To answer this question we need first to consider the nature of language use in general, since there is no other way that we can know what it is that we are being specific about. However we conceive of the objectives that learners are required to achieve on a course, these objectives are bound to be based on some kind of idealization of language use, so we need to know what it is that we are idealizing, and what different approaches to idealization leave out of account. Pedagogic presentations of language, no less than models of linguistic description, depend on theoretical decisions about relative significance. (**B** 1)

One kind of idealization involves the dissociation of linguistic forms from their communicative function in discourse. This is the typical approach of register analysis, referred to in the first chapter. A specification based on this approach will yield sets of lexical and syntactic units most commonly occurring in particular kinds of discourse. I have discussed what seem to me to be the shortcomings of such an approach elsewhere (see Discussion 5, Chapter 1). Briefly, the results of this kind of text analysis reveal what aspects of the language system most frequently accompany certain activities but not *how* they are used as an intrinsic element of these activities. We cannot know (though we may guess) how their communicative function is realized in the discourse process. It should be noted, however, that a specification based on register analysis does acknowledge the pedagogically necessary distinction between aims and objectives. It rests on the assumption that a definition of objectives in terms of linguistic items will provide for the subsequent satisfaction of communicative aims — that is to say that the imparting of linguistic competence will enable the learner to develop communicative capacity under his own steam. In this respect, it allows for learning to take place beyond the limits of the teaching input. So it is based on educational theory, even if this is not made explicit and even if we might have reason to suppose that the particular theory is in some ways mistaken.

A second kind of idealization seeks to retain the communicative value of linguistic elements and analyses language into its notional and functional meanings. This is the approach proposed by the Council of Europe in the specification of the Threshold Level and Waystage inventories, and by John Munby in developing his needs analysis instrument for communicative syllabus design. What this needs analysis approach seeks to do is to bring aims into closer approximation to objectives. In the case of Munby, indeed, it would appear that the distinction has disappeared completely, since he contends that the findings that emerge from his analysis (which characterize aims) directly determine the specification of the syllabus (which represents objectives). This, as I pointed out in the first chapter, is the orthodox view of ESP course design and it is the view that I am seeking to challenge.

The two approaches to idealization that I have referred to differ, then, in their relationship to aims and objectives. They are alike, however, in two important respects. First, they both conceive of course design as distinct from, and in principle unaffected by, methods of implementation in the actual teaching/learning process. Thus in neither case is there any suggestion that the kind of activity learners will have to be involved in when using language for their particular purposes might have implications for the kind of activity they need to be involved in in the process of learning. Specificity refers to what goes into a course and not to how it is to be taught. This is a strange omission, since it would seem on the face of it that required ways of using language might be quite closely related to preferred ways of learning language. I shall return to this matter in Chapter 3.

Meanwhile my interest in this present chapter is in the second similarity of these two approaches. It is that they are both atomistic. I mean by that that they analyse language use into constituent parts, thereby reducing the dynamic process of communication to a static inventory of items. In one case these items are of a formal linguistic kind and in the other they carry functional labels, but in both cases they are items separated out and isolated from the communicative process of which they are naturally a part. This means that at some point in learning the process has somehow to be recreated, and the items connected up with each other and recharged with dynamic life so as to become elements of language use.

It might be objected that both kinds of specification include elements of linguistic and communicative skill, so they do account for the process of language use. But the skills are also represented atomistically. In Munby's device, for example, they are itemized as a list under fifty-four different headings, each heading itself having on average five or more subheads. No hierarchy is provided and there is no way of knowing how the different skills set down separately here are actually deployed in the discourse process. It is a static list. What it records are aspects of communicative competence, kinds of knowledge that are presupposed by the ability to communicate. What is missing is any indication of what I have called the capacity to exploit this knowledge to achieve particular communicative purposes. (B 2)

What we must look for is a model of language use which does not simply atomize the user's behaviour into components of competence, but which accounts for the essential features of the discourse process. At the same time, such a model should provide us with the means of characterizing ESP at different points on the scale of specificity and be consistent with the distinctions I have proposed in the preceding chapter. The model, therefore, has to lend support to the concepts of training and education, of competence and capacity, of aims and objectives, and so give us a theoretical basis for ESP.

What I propose to do in this chapter is to put together a model which I believe satisfies these requirements. The first notion I need for this purpose is one that appears in a number of different terminological guises in the writings on discourse and artificial intelligence, and which I shall refer to as the schema. Schemata can be defined as cognitive constructs which allow for the organization of information in long-term memory and which provide a basis for prediction. They are kinds of stereotypic images which we map on to actuality in order to make sense of it, and to provide it with a coherent pattern.

Now linguistic competence is defined as a knowledge of language systems. These, I want to suggest, are second order abstractions and are not themselves projective of actual language behaviour. That is to say, we do not normally just compose or comprehend sentences so that the ability to do so has no direct executive function in language use: it is always brought in to act out an auxiliary role in the formation of utterances with appropriate communicative value. So I want to define the schema as having to do not with the structure of sentences but with the organization of utterances, as a set of expectations derived from previous experience which are projected on to instances of actual language behaviour. Consider, for example, the following:

The soldier took aim at . . .

If required to complete this expression, one's normal inclination would be to do so in something like the following way:

The soldier took aim at the target.
The soldier took aim at the enemy sentry.

But the rules of sentence formation would sanction a quite different completion as equally legitimate:

The soldier took aim at three o'clock.

The reason why the first completion comes more immediately to mind is that the resulting utterance conforms more closely to norms of expectation. The first part of the utterance activates a schema, calls up a standard context, and this is projected into the completion. (**B** 3)

The power of schemata to shape events in their own image is strong enough to override meanings explicitly signalled in the sentence if those meanings run counter to the schematic interpretation of an expression as utterance. Thus, presented with an expression like:

Don't print that or I won't sue you

people are apparently disposed to interpret and remember it as

If you print that I'll sue you.

Again, information is made to correspond with a schema representing an internalized image of a normal state of affairs. The language itself does not convey information: what it does is to provide a set of directions for which a schema in the user's mind is to be engaged. If the directions are clear, then interpretation will be a relatively straightforward affair: if they are ambiguous or otherwise non-specific, misunderstandings are likely to arise. But they arise, it must be noted, not from *sentence* ambiguity but from *utterance* ambiguity, and these are very different phenomena. Linguists have spent a good deal of time discussing the syntactic and semantic sources of ambiguous sentences like:

Visiting aunts can be boring.

Such ambiguities generally pass unnoticed, however, when they occur as utterances in contexts of use, simply because their association with other utterances in the discourse has already directed the receiver to engage a particular schema, which has the effect of filtering out any alternative interpretation. Of course, utterance ambiguity, though relatively rare, does occur and there will be occasions when clarification is called for, as in the following familiar example:

A: I think that's funny.
B: Do you mean funny peculiar or funny ha ha? (**B** 4)

There will also be occasions when the receiver is deliberately misled, when the producer of an utterance directs him to one schema and then denies him his expectation by directing him to another: the communicative equivalent of selling a dummy. Consider the following:

The blacksmith took his hammer and broke ...

what? We are led to suppose that it will be something frangible.

... his promise by throwing ...

what? Presumably the hammer.

... off all his clothes and striking ...

By this time, our predictions are in complete disarray. The events being recounted do not conform to any available schema. We cannot relate these happenings to any familiar state of affairs. Now read on:

... the pose the artist wanted. He had decided after all that he quite liked the idea of being immortalized as the god Thor. There was nothing degrading about being an artist's model.

Everything now falls into place as the scene unfolds and a schema is established which can be projected to make sense of the rest of the narrative (though destined in this case never to be written). (**B** 5)

This denial of expectation with the consequent requirement to develop an appropriate schema by retrospective construction is a particular feature of literary discourse. Indeed it follows from the very nature of literature as an art form that this should be so, since what the artist is seeking to achieve is a representation of reality which does not depend on conformity with established schemata. His aim is to avoid stock responses and to direct the receiver towards a reorganization of the patterns of experience. So the artist's purpose is served by disrupting schematic expectation and directing us to a creation of schemata which do not have the sanction of convention. Whereas other kinds of discourse converge on established schemata, literary discourse diverges from them.

A schema, then, as I have defined it here, is a stereotypic pattern derived from instances of past experience which organizes language in preparation for use. In relation to the propositional content of discourse, to what is being said, schemata can be thought of as frames of reference. In relation to the illocutionary activity of discourse, to what is being done, they may be thought of as rhetorical routines. Very commonly the collocation of particular lexical items will point to a frame of reference, and once this schema is engaged it will generate expectations about what is to come. This expectation co-exists and combines with expectation arising from the recognition of a particular rhetorical routine. Thus, for example, the words *goods, invoice, shipment, bill of lading* will direct us towards a commercial frame of reference and other expressions will be incorporated within it. If, say, *brussels sprouts* then appears, we shall already be primed to infer that the commercial enterprise concerned has to do with foodstuffs, and in particular perhaps market produce. If expressions like, say, *bromide, kangaroo, giggle,* and *urinal* were to co-occur in the same company, we would find our frame of reference incapable of containing them, and we would be obliged to look for others or to create new ones. We might suspect, for instance, that what we had to deal with here was a surrealist poem. The original set of words might also be indicative of a particular rhetorical routine, that of a business letter, and having engaged this schema we would then be prepared to look for information that needs to be acted upon.

I have said that schemata derive from past experience, and this comment needs to be elaborated upon. It has been customary, particularly among the generative linguists working within the Chomskyan paradigm, to represent language acquisition as a process of abstracting a language system, under the influence of an innate device, from an exposure to language use. The assumption seems to be that the actual circumstances of use facilitate the internalization of the system but are not themselves recorded in any way. Halliday sees the process in different terms. For him, the manner in which language functions in context has a determining effect on the actual structure of the language system itself. But these functions are, as it were, absorbed into the sentence. The sentence when used then contracts relations with the situational factors of field, mode, and style which provide it with its actualized contextual meaning. What I want to suggest is that there is a contextual level within the knowledge of language itself, a level of preparedness for use, and it is at this level that schemata have their being. So, in this view, knowledge of language embraces two levels: the level of system, where we can call it linguistic competence, and the level of schema, where we can call it communicative competence. What this proposal amounts to, in effect, is an extension of the principle of double structure or dual articulation in language. This refers to the fact that phonological systems have no direct executive function in language use but simply serve to give substantial existence to meanings signalled in syntax and semantics. What I am suggesting is a three-layer organization in which the second level of syntax and semantics has no direct executive function either, but is there to service the schematic level which is alone operative in language use. What this means is that sentences, the units at this second level, never occur in actual discourse, though they can, of course, be cited to illustrate linguistic rules.

This proposal for a third level of linguistic organization enables us, it seems to me, to explain certain phenomena which are otherwise very difficult to account for. In particular, there is the problem of expressions which are attested and interpretable but which do violence to linguistic rules. If we only have a knowledge of linguistic rules to depend upon in interpretation, how does it come about that such expressions can be interpreted without difficulty? If we postulate a schematic level, however, we can say that such expressions are not sentences at all — indeed they cannot be, by definition, since they cannot be produced by the sentence generating grammar, but are utterances interpretable by reference to the schema that has been invoked or created by the context of occurrence. Making sense of deviation proceeds in the same way as making sense of ambiguity, as illustrated earlier on in this chapter. And the same schematic operation enables us to derive significance from expressions which as sentences would be meaningless tautologies. Consider, for example, expressions like:

Boys will be boys.
Business is business.

We can make sense of such expressions only by recognizing that the formally identical lexemes on each side of the copula relate to distinct frames of reference. Of course it is true that interpretation makes use of linguistic rules, but the point is that such use is mediated through schemata. (**B** 6)

I want now to return briefly to the question of language acquisition. I said earlier that in Chomsky's view of the matter, contextual factors simply provided favourable conditions for the learning of the linguistic system, and that in Halliday's view these factors were embodied as design features of the system itself. What I would want to suggest is that as the child abstracts his linguistic rules from the mass of language data, so he also abstracts contextual outlines from the recurrent circumstances of language use and associates these outlines with linguistic realizations. So the language that is learned retains a trace of its situational provenance. Such a view seems entirely consistent with the normal process of socialization. The child's acquisition of language is often represented as if it took place in dissociation from other aspects of development, as a unique and unitary achievement. But it would surely be very surprising if this were indeed the case. While learning his language, the child is at the same time acquiring control over his environment by organizing it into conceptual categories and internalizing patterns of social behaviour. He is, in short, developing the frames of reference and routines with which he can feel secure as an individual and social being. This whole process is serviced by language, and language must also carry the imprint of this process, as Halliday suggests. But equally the schemata which result must be tagged, as it were, with the linguistic realizations which brought them about. It is difficult to accept that the child adopts the role of analyst and abstracts a linguistic system from his experience without regard to the contexts which made this system meaningful in the first place.

I would claim, then, that the assumption of a schematic level of linguistic organization has ontogenetic plausibility. It would seem to be consistent, too, with recent theory in the psychology of perception. Again it is worth making the point that a theory of language which is not congruent with what we know of other aspects of human behaviour must come under some suspicion. (**B** 7)

But schemata do not tell us the whole story of language use. They are, I have said, cognitive structures which constitute communicative competence. But I have previously talked about communicative *capacity*. How, then, is that to be accounted for?

If communication were simply a matter of applying the appropriate schema, life would be a good deal easier than it is now. It would also be almost entirely emptied of significance. There are occasions, as I have pointed out already, when one can, as it were, switch over to the automatic pilot and allow oneself to be controlled by the commonplace and the routine. Usually, however, the projection of schemata calls for negotiation, and often this will involve some modification of the schemata themselves. Without them, there is no pattern of what is given to make sense of what is new; equally, if they simply dominate and fashion all information in their own image, there can be nothing new taken in to modify what is given. Whichever way it goes, no learning can take place and, equivalently, no communication can occur. We need now to consider, then, what procedures are needed to actualize these abstract schemata in the process of discourse itself.

Interpretative procedures are needed to exploit schematic knowledge and bring it to bear on particular instances of use. All communication depends on the alignment and adjustment of each interlocutor's schemata so that they are brought into sufficient correspondence for the interlocutors to feel satisfied that they have reached an understanding. The more remote the schematic worlds of the interlocutors, the more procedural work will need to be done to achieve communicative rapport. Where schematic worlds correspond closely, procedural activity is hardly needed at all: there is no reason for lengthy negotiation when two parties agree. What does sometimes happen is that people who do not need to call on procedures to make sense of each other nevertheless feel the need to exercise their procedures and to disrupt established schemata in order to do so. As a result they become tetchy and quarrelsome, looking for the opportunity to create gaps in understanding so that they can bring their procedures to bear to bridge them.

Procedures, then, are used to match up and adjust schemata in the discourse process: they are the interactive negotiating activities which interpret the directions provided and enable us to alter our expectations in the light of new evidence as the discourse proceeds. And it is this procedural ability which realizes schematic knowledge as communicative behaviour that I refer to as capacity. This concept, therefore, covers a range of different activities which have been variously referred to as inference, practical reasoning, computing cross reference, negotiation of meaning, problem solving, and so on. It is convenient, however, to characterize them in relation to two dimensions of description. One of these has to do with the kind of schema that is being realized, that is to say whether the procedure applies to frames of reference or to rhetorical routines. The other dimension has to do with the kind of communicative situation that has to be negotiated, and in particular with the way in which the relationship between the schemata of the interlocutors is to be managed.

Before I proceed with this characterization, however, I ought to make one point clear about the distinction I have made between schematic competence and procedural capacity. Like so many distinctions of this kind, it is a convenient methodological device based on idealization. But the very nature of human language is such that the distinction cannot be absolute, since if it were it would deny language its dynamism and communicative flexibility. Schemata and procedures, and the associated abilities of competence and capacity, are best conceived of as ranged on a continuum of established convention. Thus if a particular sequence of procedures becomes so favoured by custom as to become common conventional practice, then it takes on the character of a schema and becomes part of competence. This is a familiar enough process. Consider, for example, a game like chess. If it became customary to make a certain sequence of moves at the beginning of a game so that it would be considered eccentric, even unsporting, not to conform to expectation, then these moves would in time become constitutive of a particular game of chess and the players would begin with a different disposition of pieces on the board from the one we have at present. And of course this process of change works in just the same way in language. Consider the case of a particularly inventive use of procedures which yields a metaphorical expression. This, we will suppose, is communicatively effective in that it establishes a particular frame of reference in an entirely appropriate way. Now if that expression becomes permanently attached to that frame of reference, then it will, of course, become conventionalized as part of an established schema. The metaphor then becomes part of semantic structure, and its procedural history is recorded in an etymological dictionary. So procedures not only serve to project existing schemata so that they come into focus, but they also create new ones. Sometimes, these creations will be fugitive affairs which last only as long as the discourse in which they appear; but sometimes they will be retained by custom, become conventional-ized and placed in schematic store for future use.

I return now to the characterization of procedures. The first dimension that I mentioned concerns the type of schema that the procedure works upon. Thus we have procedures which serve to establish and maintain frames of reference by tracing anaphoric reference, working out implications, and in general interpreting the given-new contract to make sense of particular instances. (**B** 8)

Consider, as example, a situation in which I have asked some-body to come to my house. He does not know just where it is but does know the location of, let us say, a certain St Mary's Church. In these circumstances I might say to him:

> You know St Mary's. Well, I live in the street on the other side of the graveyard. Number 12. It has a green gate.

My prospective guest now has procedural work to do. He has, we will assume, a frame of reference for 'church' which will include 'graveyard'. He will therefore be able to infer that the graveyard mentioned is that of the church of St Mary's. The definite article will act as a direction here, since this is always used as a pointer to a schema, whereas the possessive (*its* graveyard in this case) is used as an explicit indicator of reference within the text itself. So far, one might say, no very remarkable feat of inference is required. Elementary indeed. But now what of the pronoun *it*? Both in respect of system and schema relations, this could refer with equal likelihood to either the explicitly mentioned *graveyard* or the presupposed *house*. But to link it with the former is a fairly straightforward business: it is explicitly mentioned and it would seem to be an obvious move to match the pronoun up with it: it fits grammatically and it fits schematically, since graveyards commonly have gates. But the obvious move here is the wrong move. What my prospective guest in fact has to do to make sense of my directions is to relate the pronoun *it* not to the explicitly mentioned graveyard but to the implied referent, the house where I live. To do this he has to take bearings on this topic by referring to the expressions 'I live in the street' and 'Number 12' to come up with a schema for house (houses are located in streets and are given numbers). But this schema does not include gate. Houses have doors, not gates.

Garden, however, is part of the house schema and gardens do have gates, so that it can be inferred that *it* refers to gate, which links to garden, which links to house, which links to the place on the street where I live. So the inference required here is not so elementary. Of course, analysing it out in this way makes it appear a more cumbersome operation than it would actually be. Analysis often has this distorting effect when applied to mental processes. So I would not wish to suggest that my prospective guest has to plod through the reasoning that I have represented here in any explicit way. We develop a capacity for very nimble mental activity in making sense in discourse. What I have tried to spell out is the kind of procedures involved.

There are occasions, it might be worth pointing out, however, when we are required to go through our procedures consciously: this is the case when it is not at all clear what the frame of reference is and we have to plot it by a careful sifting of the given evidence. Sometimes the directions are quite deliberately inexplicit, as in riddles, where the whole point of the game is to discover the hidden frame of reference. Once the schema is traced, the clues fall immediately into place and we wonder how we could have missed something so obvious.

So much (for the moment at any rate) for procedures which make sense of propositional information by relating it to schemata which define frames of reference. I turn now to procedures which realize rhetorical routines. Like frames of reference, routines are hierarchically organized. Just as, for example, the house frame is included within the town frame, so a routine which defines a particular illocutionary act can be contained within a larger routine, or macro-act, if you will, or speech event. So we may begin with the illocutionary act. This is defined by a set of conditions which interlocutors have to acknowledge as realized within a particular situation. But it may, of course, not be at all clear that the situation does provide for a satisfactory realization of these conditions, or one interlocutor may wish to alter the situation in some way so that it does not provide for them. And this is where procedures come in.

A standard illustration of how interpretative procedures are applied to realize illocutionary value is an exchange of the following kind:

A: I have two tickets for the theatre tonight.
B: My examination is tomorrow.
A: Pity. (**B** 9)

Here, B, we may assume, recognizes that A's utterance keys in with situational factors in such a way as to make the utterance interpretable as an invitation. She supposes that A is working on the same assumption, that both of them are making implicit reference to the routine conditions of invitation, that it does not make sense to suppose that A is simply providing her with gratuitous information. Furthermore, she knows that it is routine behaviour to respond to an invitation by either acceptance or refusal, and she assumes that A knows that, too. Her own utterance, in these circumstances, is interpretable as a refusal of the invitation, and A's following remark makes it clear that it is so interpreted. But there is a further feature of this routine that needs to be taken into account: and that is that if an invitation is refused, it is customary to provide some kind of excuse which will justify it. Unless B were a particularly rude sort of person, or unless there were factors in the situation which warranted abruptness, it would be surprising if the exchange had taken the following form:

A: I have two tickets for the theatre tonight.
B: No.

So B's response:

B: My examination is tomorrow

is intended and interpreted as an excuse, and since one cannot just produce an excuse unrelated to a course of action, proposed or in the past, it is related to refusal. And so A and B make sense of their utterances by referring them to the shared routines which represent a part of their common communicative competence.

Of course, things might not have worked out so smoothly. So far I have been discussing the way procedures work in drawing silent conclusions from conversational data. But this mental operation can be realized as overt social behaviour, and then meanings are negotiated by reciprocal interaction. The exchange between A and B might, after all, have gone like this:

A: I have two tickets for the theatre tonight.
B: Good for you. What are you going to see?
A: *Measure for Measure.*
B: Interesting play. Hope you enjoy it.

Assuming that A's utterance was intended as an invitation, the conversation is not going according to plan, so he has to negotiate a return to his intended purpose:

A: Look, are you free tonight?
B: I am not sure. Why?

A is still not getting his message across and at this point he may feel that explicitness is the best policy:

A: Well, I would like to invite you to come to the theatre with me.
B: Well, actually, my examination is tomorrow.

Now it might be A's turn to be obtuse by not recognizing the remark as an excuse and so not reading B's remark as a refusal:

A: I know, so is mine. What's that got to do with it?

And so on.

So these procedures of making sense, whether in relation to routines or frames of reference, many operate covertly or may be realized as overt interaction between interlocutors, depending on how much shared schematic knowledge can be presupposed and how far the nonlinguistic factors in the situation are a reliable support to what is actually expressed in the utterance.

Procedural negotiation, then, can be quite protracted on occasions, as intentions miss their mark, directions go astray, and the necessary schemata are not engaged. Interlocutors will sometimes decide that the point of an interaction does not warrant such expense of time and patience and will disengage, drawing unfavourable conclusions (overtly or covertly) about the other person's intelligence or integrity. This happens frequently in interethnic interaction, which calls for particularly intensive procedural activity to bridge the gap between schemata which are very different. Sometimes interlocutors will seek to clarify their meanings by shifting to a different signalling system altogether, from a linguistic to a pictorial mode of presenting information. Thus, if I find that verbal directions do not get my message across to my prospective guest, I can draw him a map indicating the church, the graveyard, my house: a diagrammatic frame of reference. This kind of schematic representation is very common in certain kinds of discourse: a fact which is of considerable relevance to ESP, as we shall see later when the discussion in this chapter is referred back to issues raised in Chapter 1.

Since the negotiation in establishing a frame of reference or a routine may be lengthy, there is always the possibility that it may so occupy the interlocutors' attention that the objective of the negotiation may be lost sight of. There is a need in this case for recapitulation, resumé, a drawing together of the threads. Such a procedure can be referred to as a *formulation*. The overt indicators of such a procedure are expressions like:

Where were we?
So what you are saying is . . .
Now let's get this straight.
Are you trying to tell me that . . .?

And so on. And just as we have two kinds of procedure corresponding to the two kinds of schemata — frames of reference and rhetorical routines — so we have, logically enough, two kinds of formulation. One of these recapitulates propositional content and makes clear what frame of reference has been negotiated: this we will refer to as the formulation of *gist*. The other formulation recapitulates illocutionary intent and makes clear what routine has been negotiated: we can refer to this as the formulation of *upshot*. (**B** 10)

In relation to the exchanges already considered, my prospective guest might produce a gist of the sort:

So your house is opposite the graveyard.

With regard to A and B, locked in the business of inviting and refusing, the following upshots might be produced:

A: Look, I am inviting you to come to the theatre.
B: I'm sorry, but I have to refuse.

Alternatively, upshots might come from the initiator of the routine, rather than from the interpreter:

B: Is that an invitation?
A: Are you turning me down?

Gists and upshots, then, focus on the main point of an interaction, propositional on the one hand, illocutionary on the other. But why, one might ask, do interlocutors not get to the point in the first place and avoid all this procedural obfuscation? This question brings us to the second way of considering these procedures, mentioned earlier in this chapter.

Schemata, as I have defined them, are cognitive structures which the individual uses to organize experience. They represent his security: with them he can make sense of, and so in some degree control, events that impinge on him from the outside. They both create and protect the domain of his own experiential territory. But at the same time, of course, he cannot simply seal himself off from the outside world, because he depends upon it as a social being. His own universe has to engage with that of others and be subjected to continual change. This means that human communication involves the reconciliation of two opposing forces. One is a function of the territorial imperative, as powerful in humans as in other species of animal, which disposes the individual to maintain his own schematic life space against the threat of invading influence. The other is a function of the co-operative imperative which disposes the individual to assume a social role, for his own good, and to accept a modification to his world in return for social benefits. Survival depends on getting right the balance between these two forces. There is, fortunately, room for manoeuvre. You can be temperamentally inclined towards maintaining your territory, and in this case you will be inclined to be an introvert. But only in extreme instances of hermits who devote their lives to silence in isolation does this result in a total denial of the co-operative imperative. Conversely, you may be blessed with so much confidence in your own security that you allow the co-operative imperative to dominate your behaviour. Your inclination will then be extrovert. But again even the most extreme extrovert usually has a secure line of communication back to his own individual domain and will return to base when under serious threat.

It is the co-operative imperative which impels people to put their schemata into contact with others, and there are procedures available to service this impulse. These co-operative procedures are concerned with making information *accessible*, with clarifying its relationship with existing schemata, building up frames of reference, indicating which routine is in operation and so on, all the time working towards a satisfactory convergence of worlds so that understanding can be achieved.

But communication is not only a matter of making intentions clear, or understanding the intentions of others. If understanding is, as I have argued, dependent on the engagement of the individual's personal construct of reality, then access to it could be seen as intrusion. In order to be co-operative, one has to encroach on somebody else's life space and leave one's own vulnerable to invasion. The territorial imperative has also to be respected. So it is that many of the procedures we use are protective and are directed at ensuring that what is said is not only accessible but also *acceptable* to others. It is all very well to believe in being blunt and plain-spoken, but to be so is to rely on a tolerance that many people might be reluctant to extend, and they are likely, in this case, to disengage from the interaction. Communication depends on interlocutors being receptive, and this means that both propositional information and illocutionary intent has to be expressed in such a way that it is both accessible and acceptable. In other words, procedures have to service both the co-operative and the territorial imperatives. (**B** 11)

The reason, therefore, why A in the exchange we have been considering does not issue an invitation directly to B is likely to be because he wishes to protect himself from a rebuff. So he approaches tentatively and gives an indirect indication of his intent. In this way, he can save face in the event of refusal by disclaiming his original intention. For example:

A: I have two tickets for the theatre tonight.
B: Sorry, I can't go.
A: Well, actually, I wasn't going to invite you. I'm going with Cynthia.

Acceptability procedures operate here to implement illocutionary intent. But they can also operate on propositional information. I may wish to draw attention to something I believe to be already known to my interlocuter, although I may not be absolutely sure. So I want to make sure, without seeming to insult his intelligence by stating the obvious. I therefore employ expressions like 'of course', which indicate an assumption of shared knowledge, or 'as you know', even if I am pretty sure that the person addressed does not know:

Of course, the government has already committed funds for that purpose. As you know, the committee has no constitutional status.

Similarly, acceptability procedures are brought into play when the information to be conveyed is disagreeable (I'm afraid you are not going to like this, but . . .) or hard to credit (You won't believe this, but . . .)

These protective procedures are of course more in evidence in some kinds of situation than in others. There are occasions when accessibility is at a premium and acceptability criteria in suspense. In certain kinds of service encounter, for example, it is accepted that business is to be carried out as briskly as possible, since its conduct does not impinge on the personal territory of those concerned. An example:

A: Return to Waterloo, please.
B: One ninety.

With a long queue of people behind me about to miss their train, I do not waste time in polite social chat. All I have to do is give direct expression to the routine. The same is true of the following:

A: Do you have any Briteclean toothpaste?
B: 55p.

The shopkeeper knows the routine as well as I do and takes no offence at its most economical realization. He knows that in this situation my most operative utterance will indicate what I wish to buy, and will be a request for action on his part (viz. fetching the article mentioned). He is therefore able to interpret my first remark not as a request for information only, but as a request for action. I am counting on its being a sufficient direction for him to invoke the required routine. However, if I had time and inclination and the shopkeeper did too, the exchange could take on a different form:

A: Good morning.
B: Good morning. Lovely day.
A: Delightful. What can I do for you?
B: Do you, I wonder, have any Briteclean toothpaste?
A: Yes, I believe we do.
B: Could I have two tubes, please?
A: Two tubes? Certainly. That will be £1.10, please.

and so on.

It is time to formulate the gist of this present chapter, to do a summary sketch of the model of language use I am proposing. I am suggesting that there is a level of language competence which consists of stereotypic, skeletal structures of language use which I have called schemata. These develop in acquisition as the child associates the lexical and syntactic elements with recurrent patterns of their occurence. They are used to project an order on experience and to provide for the orderly management of new information. These schemata take the form of frames of reference for propositional content and rhetorical routines for illocutionary intent, and their engagement allows the user to anticipate the development of discourse and to make sense of it. This engagement is effected by means of procedures of various kinds. These mediate between the schemata of the interlocutors involved in the discourse interaction. Where these schemata are very different, a good deal of procedural activity will be required; where they are very similar, procedural activity will be minimal. Procedures are necessary not only to relate and extend schemata so that what is being said is made accessible, both in regard to its propositional content and illocutionary intent, but also to ensure that this connection of different individual worlds is achieved without seeming to trespass on and threaten the security of the personal domain. So procedures have to be concerned both with accessibility and acceptability, have to maintain an equilibrium between the two potentially opposing forces of the territorial imperative on the one hand, which provides for individual security, and the co-operative imperative on the other, which provides for the need for social interaction.

It is this ability to realize and modify existing schemata by the use of such procedures that I refer to as 'capacity'. It is capacity which enables us to exploit the language system as a meaning resource by relating it to our schematic knowledge of the conventions of language use, and so to actualize the interaction of the discourse process, whether enacted in speech or writing.

But how does all this relate to ESP? What I must do next is to demonstrate the relevance of the model of language use I have developed in this chapter to the issues on the aims and objectives in ESP that I raised in the first.

B   Discussion

1.   *Idealization*

All systematic enquiry requires some measure of idealization whereby abstract patterns are derived from actual instances. In this respect, systematic enquiry is simply an extension of the basic principle of language itself, which seeks to account for reality, and so control it, by organizing it into verbal categories.

As far as the linguist is concerned, the abstract patterns which are the subject of his enquiry are the permissible combinations of linguistic signs made manifest by sentences. Such patterns constitute the underlying system of a language which is realized in utterances, the particular instances of actual language behaviour.

Lyons has suggested (Lyons 1972) that in order to establish this system, to derive abstract sentences from actual utterances, the linguist needs to subject his data to three kinds of process: regularization, standardization, and decontextualization. The first of these dispenses with irregularities of expression contingent on the circumstances of utterance: hesitations, repetitions, false starts, self editing, and so on. The second disregards variation and makes an assumption of homogeneity: that is to say, it is supposed for the purpose of description that linguistic expressions conform to a stable (if not static) and well-defined system. The third process removes linguistic expressions from their context of occurrence and treats them as isolates, related only to other isolates as terms in this system.

The language teacher must, of course, also idealize his data in some way. He cannot simply expose his students to the raw data of natural language use. It has been commonly assumed in the past that the linguist's idealization will serve the purpose, that the sentence is the unit of language teaching just as it is the unit of language analysis. It seems on the face of it quite natural to suppose that the discipline of linguistics ought to be the source of content for the subject of language teaching. There are, however, problems about this supposition.

We should note to begin with that the linguist, by the process of decontextualization, cuts language off from its connection with natural circumstances of use. The linguistic unit that is thereby derived is a formal abstraction which can, as such, only be cited and not actually used. Now such a unit can, of course, be 're-contextualized' by contriving a classroom situation of some kind, but if that situation is set up simply to demonstrate the meaning of the unit, then that unit will retain its character as a sentence. If it is to occur as an utterance, then the decontextualization process has to be reversed in some way; the linguist's idealization cannot be retained. The provision of situations to demonstrate the sentences of usage is not at all the same as the presentation of utterances in the natural contexts of language use (see Widdowson 1978 Chapter 1).

This point can be made in relation to the nature of the linguistic sign. The linguist's idealization of data established the sign as *symbol*. This has meaning by virtue of the fact that it denotes types of event, entity, experience, etc., abstracted from actuality, and contracts sense relations with other symbols as terms within the language system. Thus the meaning of symbols is constant and self-contained. The following combination of symbols, constituting a sentence

The fishermen are mending their nets

has a quite specific meaning because of its sense and denotation. This meaning can be computed by checking what the symbols 'fisherman', 'mend', and 'net' denote and establishing that 'are mending' expounds a term in the tense/aspect system of English and so has a particular sense relation with other terms in that system like 'were mending', 'mended', and so on. It is the business of semantics to describe the principles of computation of this kind which accounts for symbolic meaning.

The study of symbols depends on separating linguistic expressions from their context of occurrence. In their natural surroundings *in* context, these expressions constitute a very different kind of sign. They no longer operate as symbols but as *indices*. They indicate where meaning is to be found beyond themselves in the context in which they occur. In the case of the fishermen and their nets, for example, we would need to identify the particular fishermen referred to. Whereas the sentence has symbolic meaning by virtue of sense and denotation, the utterance has indexical meaning which has to be achieved by the language user by referring to the particular context of its occurrence.

If language teaching is to be concerned with language use, then, it cannot be entirely based on the linguist's idealization of data which is concerned with the decontextualized sign as symbol.

My use of the terms *symbol* and *index* derives from the distinction drawn by C. S. Peirce as discussed in Lyons 1977: 99–109. However, as Lyons shows, the distinction is far from clear in Peirce's writings, and I have taken advantage of this to impose my own interpretation on these terms, as others have done before me. For me, then, the symbol is a unit of semantic meaning with a specifiable *sense* and *denotation*, whereas the index is a unit of pragmatic meaning used for the act of *reference*.

2. Itemization of skills

The effect of itemizing skills (or language forms or functions) as an inventory of isolates is to deny their dynamic inter-relationship in the actuality of behaviour. Consider the following extracts from Munby:

1 Discriminating sounds in isolate word forms.
   1.1 phonemes, especially phonemic contrasts.
   etc.

2 Articulating sounds in isolate word forms.
   2.1 phonemes, especially phonemic contrasts.
   etc.
3 Discriminating sounds in connected speech.
   3.1 strong and weak forms.
   etc.

24 Understanding conceptual meaning, especially
   24.1 quantity and amount.
   etc.
25 Expressing conceptual meaning, especially
   25.1 quantity and amount.
   etc.
26 Understanding the communicative value (function) of sentences
   and utterances.
   26.1 with explicit indicators.
   etc.

30 Understanding relations between parts of a text through lexical
   cohesion devices of
   30.1 repetition
   etc.

34 Interpreting text by going outside it,
   34.1 using exophoric reference
   34.2 'reading between the lines'
   34.3 integrating data in the text with own experience or
       knowledge of the world

(Munby 1978: 123–8)

The items listed under 1–3 here are lower level automatic skills which are generally deployed without awareness in the normal circumstances of language use. They are skills in the strict sense, as defined in the previous chapter (Discussion 7). They need to be pushed down below the level of consciousness since they would otherwise interfere with the higher order skills (which I have referred to as abilities) itemized under 24–26, 30 and 34. There is, therefore, a hierarchy here which is crucial to the characterization of skills but which is not given any recognition in this inventory. Consider now the higher order skills (or abilities) as applied, let us to say, in the act of reading. To understand conceptual meaning (24) will usually involve the understanding of the communicative function of utterances (26) which in turn cannot be done without relating one part of the text to another (30) and parts of the text with one's own knowledge of the world (34). In other words, these 'skills' have an implicational relationship with each other so that the acquisition and use of one presupposes the acquisition and use of others.

Munby calls his list a taxonomy, but in the usual sense of that term it is not a taxonomy at all:

> ... we subjectively group the phenomena of our perceptual world into name classes. These classes are not disparate and singular. They are organized into larger groupings. To the extent that these groupings are hierarchically arranged by a process of inclusion, they form a taxonomy. (Tyler 1969: 7)

The point, then, is that a serial itemization of the kind provided by Munby misrepresents the essential nature of skills and abilities. Their inter-relations are lost in the list.

For a discussion of skill theory in relation to language learning, see Levelt 1975, McDonough 1981: Chapter 3.

3.   Schemata

The concept of the schema was proposed fifty years ago by the psychologist F. C. Bartlett (Bartlett 1932) to account for the way information in stories is refashioned in memory so as to make it consistent with custom. In Bartlett's experiments, people were told an American Indian story and asked to reproduce it. The story, *The war of the ghosts*, expressed beliefs and followed narrative conventions which were strange to the British students who acted as subjects in the experiments, and in their versions they adjusted the original content to make it correspond more closely to their own way of looking at the world. In other words, they interpreted the content by fitting it into their own frames of reference, their own schemata.

Schemata, then can be defined as cognitive constructs or configurations of knowledge which we place over events so as to bring them into alignment with familiar patterns of experience and belief. They therefore serve as devices for categorizing and arranging information so that it can be interpreted and retained.

The idea of the schema has assumed particular importance over recent years in the fields of artificial intelligence and cognitive science, and there has been a good deal of experimentation and speculation about the structure of particular schemata and how they work in the processes of understanding and memorization. See, for example, the collections of papers in Bobrow and Collins

1975, Just and Carpenter 1977, Freedle 1977. For an account of how these fields of enquiry impinge on the study of text and discourse, see Beaugrande and Dressler 1981.

The investigation of the general concept of the schema as a cognitive representation of normal patterns of reality has led to various refinements and distinctions, accompanied inevitably by a confusing proliferation of different terms. The most commonly occurring seem to be: frame, script, scenario, and plan.

When a field of enquiry lacks the stability of an established paradigm, as discourse studies do at the present, there is always a good deal of terminological groping for clarity. There is not even agreement on what this field of enquiry should be called: it is variously known as discourse analysis, text linguistics, pragmalinguistics. In such circumstances of uncertainty, it is difficult to decide whether different terms mark significant conceptual distinctions or are simply a matter of idiosyncratic preference. In the present case, however, it does seem as if these terms relating to the schema can be justified on the grounds that they denote different aspects of schematic organization, as Beaugrande tries to make clear (Beaugrande 1980: Chapter VI)

There is, to begin with, a legitimate distinction to be made between patterns of conceptual organization and patterns of participation in social life. The first kind are related to the ideational function of language and the second to the interpersonal function. Halliday has shown how these functions are formalized in the abstract linguistic systems of transitivity and mood (Halliday 1973). If we take the term 'schema' as a superordinate denoting configurations of knowledge in general, we may say that we have ideational schemata on the one hand and interpersonal schemata on the other. It is the former that van Dijk would appear to have in mind when he talks about frames:

> The concept . . . denotes (sic) a conceptual structure in semantic memory and represents a part of our knowledge of the world. In this respect a frame is an ORGANIZATIONAL PRINCIPLE, relating a number of concepts which by CONVENTION and EXPERIENCE somehow form a 'unit' which may be actualized in various cognitive tasks, such as language production and comprehension, perception, action, and problem solving. Thus, in a RESTAURANT-frame would be organized the conventional, i.e. general but culture dependent, knowledge that a restaurant is a building or place where one eats publicly, where food is either

ordered from a waiter/waitress or taken at a counter, etc. That is,
a frame organizes knowledge about certain properties of objects,
courses of event and action which TYPICALLY belong together.
(van Dijk 1977a: 159)

This knowledge about objects, events, actions, and so on is derived,
as Halliday puts it, from:

... the speaker's experience of the external world, and of his
own internal world, that of his own consciousness.
(Halliday 1979: 45)

And it is given abstract formalization in the language system itself.
van Dijk's frames are clearly the schematic analogue of Halliday's
transitivity systems. They represent ideational knowledge at the
schematic level of language organization.

The interpersonal schema corresponding to the ideational frame
is the *plan* or *script*, as discussed, for example, in Schank and
Abelson 1977. The plan is represented as a sequence of goal-
directed actions, and the script as a conventionalized version
established as a routine, a predictable situational sequence. Schank
and Abelson, for example, analyse a RESTAURANT-script (cf. van
Dijk's RESTAURANT-frame) into four scenes: entering, ordering,
eating, exiting, each one of which is further broken down into
constituent acts. These acts are for the most part physical *actions*
like PTRANS: transfer of physical location of object, or PROPEL:
application of physical force to object; but some involve communicative interactivity, notably MTRANS: transfer of mental
information between or within animals. In the restaurant script this
would take the form of speech acts of various kinds like calling the
waiter, asking for the menu, ordering, and so on. The concept of
the script, therefore, allows in principle for the characterization of
conventional sequences of speech acts, or rhetorical routines. This
being so, we can see how the work of Schank and Abelson in
Artificial Intelligence relates to that done by Sinclair and Coulthard
on the structure of classroom discourse (Sinclair and Coulthard
1975). The essential difference between them is that Schank and
Abelson are concerned with the speech situation as a whole,
whereas Sinclair and Coulthard concentrate on the speech event, as
these terms are used by Hymes:

Speech situation
Within a community one readily detects many situations associated with (or marked by the absence of) speech. Such contexts of

situation will often be naturally described as ceremonies, fights, hunts, meals, lovemaking, and the like ... The term *speech event* will be restricted by activities, or aspects of activities, that are directly governed by rules or norms for the use of speech. (Hymes 1974: 51–2)

Since scripts are clearly intended as abstract representations of speech situations rather than speech events, I shall use the term *routine* to refer to interpersonal schemata corresponding to mood at the level of system in a Hallidaian grammar.

The only term that remains undefined is *scenario*. It is used as a central concept in Sanford and Garrod's excellent account of the schematic character of written discourse. Their definition of the term is not, however, very enlightening:

The scenario is an information network called from long-term memory by a particular linguistic input ...
(Sanford and Garrod 1981: 127)
... representations of situations or events from long-term memory. (ibid: 115)
... a model of a recognizable episode or situation ... (ibid: 117)

One may infer from the discussion, however, that what these authors seem to have in mind is a combination of frame and routine. That is to say, a network of conceptual associations tied in with a co-occurring sequence of acts constituting a conventional episode or event.

As such, it closely parallels Firth's notion of the context of situation. It is true that Firth sees this as a device for linguistic description rather than as a principle in discourse processing on the part of the language user, but it is clear that he conceived of it as a schema, with ideational and interpersonal aspects, very much along the lines we have been discussing. Consider, for example:

My view was, and still is, that 'context of situation' is best used as a suitable *schematic construct* to apply to language events, and that it is a group of related categories at a *different level from grammatical categories but rather of the same abstract nature*. (Firth 1957: 182) (My emphasis)

The view I am putting forward in this book, then, is that there are two basic levels of language knowledge, the systemic and the schematic, and that it is the second that serves as the main source of reference in language use. The two levels represent different ways of structuring the main functions of language. In language use, the systemic level is not directly engaged, but provides resources for sustaining the schematic level when required. With regard to the distinction between types of sign introduced in Discussion 1, the symbol operates at the systemic level and the index operates at the schematic level.

On a very general schematic level, Eugene Winter has made the interesting suggestion that there is a basic rhetorical routine underlying discourse structure which consists of two related parts, *problem* and *solution*, together with a *situation*, which provides the setting for the problem, and an *evaluation*, which provides an assessment of the effects of the solution. We have therefore a four part sequence, which Winter illustrates by the following invented example:

I was on sentry duty.   — Situation
I saw the enemy approaching.   — Problem
I opened fire.   — Solution
I beat off the enemy attack.   — Evaluation

The claim is not that all discourse conforms invariably to this schema, but that this represents the normal or unmarked sequence which serves as a point of reference and a basis for anticipation. See Winter 1976, Hoey 1979.

In the field of ESP, the work of Selinker and the Trimbles on the rhetorical structure of technical writing in English can be seen as the description of scenarios in the Sanford and Garrod sense, in that they are concerned with how certain illocutionary acts (reporting, defining, etc.) are combined, and how they are related to ways of organizing propositional information (see Lackstrom, Selinker and Trimble 1973, Selinker, Trimble and Trimble 1978). They outline what they call a 'Rhetorical Process Chart'. This comprises four levels of hierarchical organization, as follows:

Level A   *The objectives of the total discourse*
          e.g. Detailing an experiment
               Presenting new hypotheses or theories
               etc.
Level B   *The general rhetorical functions employed to develop the
          objectives of Level A*
          e.g. Stating purpose
               Reporting past research
               etc.

Level C   *The specific rhetorical functions employed to develop the*
           objectives of Level B
           e.g. Definition
                Classification
                etc.
Level D   *The rhetorical techniques that provide relationships*
           within and between the units of Level C
           e.g. Time order
                Causality
                etc.

If one could establish an implicational relationship across particular elements in each level so that one could say for a particular kind of discourse that Level A unit X constrained a certain combination of units from Level B, which in turn constrained selection and ordering from Level C and ultimately from Level D, then we could use a chart of this kind to characterize the scenarios which identify particular genres or schematic types (see also Swales 1981a, referred to again in Discussion 4 Chapter 3).

Notice that it is not clear from this chart, as it is not clear in discourse studies generally, how far elements of the Level D sort are different in kind from those that appear in the upper levels. They are referred to as 'rhetorical techniques' as distinct from the 'rhetorical functions' of Levels C and B. I would tend to associate the former with frame and the latter with routine structure, having made this distinction in line with Searle's division of the proposition and the illocution in the individual speech act (cf. Searle 1969). However, it has to be recognized that there are interdependencies between them (as there are interdependencies within the language system between syntax and semantics) which make it difficult to keep them apart. The routine of process description, for example, involves time order frame structure; classification calls for comparison and contrast; explanation requires a reference to causality. These are necessary propositional conditions on the performance of these various illocutionary acts. Establishing these conditions brings ideational and interpersonal schemata into convergence and defines the elements of a particular scenario.

4. Ambiguity

Whereas the sentence, by definition, signals its own meaning in dissociation from any context (see Discussion 1 in this Chapter), the indexical signs of the utterance will always direct the interpreter to some context or other. Thus, confronted with the expression:

Don't print that or I won't sue you

people will treat it indexically and engage a normal frame of reference, thereby over-riding the symbolic meaning of the syntax. As Fillenbaum puts it (whose example this is), people will resort to 'pragmatic normalization' (Fillenbaum 1973). There is an obvious parallel between this normalization and the adjustments made by the subjects in Bartlett's experiments to the information in the stories they were told (see Discussion 3).

In the case of this Fillenbaum example, then, what we have is a disparity between symbolic and indexical meaning, and where this occurs it will generally be the latter which prevails. Consider now the question of ambiguity. This is commonly exemplified by expressions like the one cited here:

1. Visiting aunts can be boring.

We are told that this is an ambiguous *sentence*, on the grounds that it is open to two distinct interpretations and can be related, therefore, to two distinct underlying structures. These can be indicated by the glosses:

Aunts who visit can be boring.
To visit aunts can be boring.

The claim, then, is that ambiguity is a function of the convergence of *symbolic* meanings. In fact, however, what is illustrated by expressions such as these is a convergence of *indexical* meanings so that as utterances isolated from any context which would resolve the matter they call up schemata of equal likelihood: going to visit aunts on the one hand and receiving visits from aunts on the other. Consider now the following expressions:

2. Visiting lecturers can be boring.
3. Visiting sick people can be boring.

Compared with the first example (1), these are equally ambiguous — as *sentences*. There is nothing whatever in the symbolic meaning of the terms *lecturer* and *sick people* which would preclude the specification of the underlying structures:

To visit lecturers can be boring.
Sick people who visit can be boring.

What prevents us from recognizing the ambiguity of (2) and (3) (and what prevents linguists from citing them as instances of ambiguity) is that as utterances, as indexical expressions, they fail to engage a schema associated with a normal state of affairs. To put it another way, they do not suggest two contexts of likely occurrence, but only one. So when they claim to be exemplifying sentence ambiguity, linguists actually make appeal to indexical meaning, which has nothing to do with sentences as such.

5. *Schematic anticipation*

Schematic knowledge is not only engaged to process incoming information by relating it retrospectively to established patterns, it also works prospectively to project anticipations about what is to come. It is for this reason that we can learn to read with such rapidity, particularly when the content and its manner of organization is familiar: the act of reading does not involve so much the accumulation of new knowledge as the *confirmation* of predictions based on what is already known. We bring to reading, as we do to all experience of language use, what Frank Smith calls 'the theory of the world in the head' (see Smith 1978: Chapter 5) and this theory leads us to set up hypotheses, or in my terms schematic projections, to be tested as further information comes in from the discourse process.

If anticipations based on schematic projection are denied, if our theories fail, then there will be a disruption of normality which will call for a rapid reappraisal of our schematic projections, or what T. S. Eliot refers to as 'stock responses'. It is, of course, precisely such reappraisal that literature (and all art) seeks to encourage. So it is that literary writers deliberately flout the conventions upon which other forms of discourse depend (see Widdowson 1975).

Sanford and Garrod (1981) give the following example of the denial of schematic anticipation:

> John was on his way to school last Friday —
> He was really worried about the maths lesson —
> Last week he had been unable to control the class —
> It was unfair of the maths teacher to leave him in charge —
> After all, it is not a normal part of the janitor's duties.

They comment:

> To the extent that such an example is disturbing, it illustrates the fact that the text evokes a model of a situation which is based on the knowledge the reader already has.
> (Sanford and Garrod 1981: 10)

This model is what they later define as a *scenario*, a schematic construct (see Discussion 2, this chapter). The reader is disturbed because he has to keep changing his frame of reference, and cannot settle into secure predictions.

6.   *Tautology and metaphor*

Lyons makes the following comments on tautologies such as these:

> It is important to realize that, although the particular interpretation given to such utterances may vary from context to context, the meaning of the sentence itself is constant. There is no need to invoke any notion of metaphor or connotative meaning in order to account for their interpretability. What the addressee does, upon hearing and understanding a tautologous utterance, is to say to himself, as it were, 'There must be some reason for the speaker to tell me what he knows I know to be true. What can this reason be?' The addressee assumes, in default of any evidence to the contrary, that the speaker is not indulging in irrelevant platitudes. (Lyons 1977: 417)

No doubt it will usually be the case that in accordance with what Grice (1975) calls the co-operative principle (of which more later) the addressee will assume that the speaker intends his utterance to be informative in some way. But this does not explain *how* expressions of this tautologous sort can be construed so as to be informative; it simply states that they are so construed.

Such expressions do not have to depend on their appearance in context to be interpreted as utterances, and indeed it is doubtful if a context would give very much guidance. The point is that since we cannot make sense of them as sentences, we shift our attention from the systemic to the schematic level, treat them as utterances and look for a likely indexical meaning. Thus, as a sentence

Boys will be boys

contains no more meaning than do the sentences

Books will be books
Toys will be toys
etc.

The words on each side of the copula 'will be' have in each case the same denotation, are tokens of the same symbol, and in consequence the sentence has no semantic content. It is not meaning, but its absence, which is constant. But although these particular combinations of symbols signal tautologies without meaning, we can make something of the combination of indices in the utterance. Working on the assumption that utterances like these are intended to be informative, we try to realize different indexical meanings for the two repeated words by associating them with different frames of reference. Our success in doing this depends on the extent to which there are conventional frames of reference to refer to.

How is this realization of indexical meaning achieved? We may begin by the explanation that is offered by Sacks (1972) to account for the coherence of the following:

The baby cried. The mommy picked it up.

Sacks points out that the term 'baby' belongs to two different 'membership categorization devices', by which he means what I have called ideational schemata or frames of reference. One of these is the 'family' device, where the term keeps company with other terms like, for example, 'mommy', 'daddy' and so on; and the other schematic device is 'stage of life' where 'baby' is associated with 'child', 'teenager', 'adult', and so on. Now Sacks says that there is a maxim (derived actually from the general Gricean co-operative principle — see Discussion 11 below) which constrains the interpreter to associate two expressions with the same device. In the case of his own example, therefore, the interpreter would be inclined to select from the two indexical interpretations available for 'baby' ('family' and 'stage of life') the one which engages the device or frame of reference which also includes the term 'mommy', i.e. 'family'.

Turning now to our example:
Boys[1] will be boys.[2]

It is clear that we can understand this as a meaningful utterance only if we are able to associate each occurrence of 'boys' with a different schematic device, or frame of reference. That is to say, we have to give each of them a different indexical value. Whereas as symbols these terms are tokens of the same type, as indices they are tokens of different types. So we might associate boy^1 with physiological features which define a frame we might call 'physical growth', and boy^2 with certain behavioural and attitudinal characteristics which define what we might call a 'psychological maturation' frame. Thus we can interpret the expression in something like the following way:

Boys (people at a particular age) will be boys (will behave in a particular way).

For example:

Boys will be boisterous, noisy, untidy, etc.

The reason that we are able to make good sense of this apparent tautology without any difficulty is that we have conventional warrant for both schemata. It is the second of them (psychological maturation), for example, that is engaged to make sense of expressions like 'behaving like one of the boys'. The word 'toys', on the other hand, is not indexical of two different frames of reference and so it is harder to make meaning out of it.

The striking effect of tautology depends on our recognizing that although two terms are tokens of the same symbol in the sentence, they are distinguishable as indices in the utterance, in that they can refer us to two frames of reference. What then happens, one might ask, when a similar convergence of distinct frames is symbolically marked, where schematic realignment results in systemic change, and therefore violates established syntactic or semantic rule? The answer is: metaphor. In making sense of metaphor, as in making sense of tautology, our attention is drawn to a relationship between schemata which is not self evident: either because indexical differences are not symbolically marked (as in tautology) or because the symbolic system provides only a codified abstraction of schemata which are conventionally sanctioned (as in metaphor). Consider, for example, the following:

Business is business.

When they wage business there are no survivors.

We can indicate their meanings in the following way:

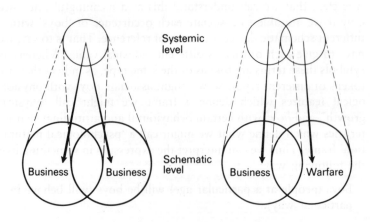

Here the circles in the foreground represent schemata, those in the background symbols at the systemic level. Indexical meaning is the projection from the background to the foreground (marked by arrows). The area of overlap of the foreground circles reflects the degree of schematic similarity so that the less overlap there is, the more difficult it will be to give the metaphor or the tautology a meaningful interpretation.

I would argue, then, that metaphors and tautologies are closely related phenomena and both have to do with the realization of indexical meaning, or with what Lyons and other semanticists sometimes refer to as *connotation*. In my scheme of things, connotation is the indication of the covert schematic context of an utterance which it projects out of isolation. When this is realized in contexts of actual occurrence, it takes the overt form of *collocation*. I see these, therefore, not as different 'types' of meaning (cf. Leech 1981: Chapter 2), but as different functions of the linguistic sign as index in the utterance.

7. Perception

It seems logical to suppose that the perception of meaning as indicated by linguistic signs ought to follow the same essential principles as the perception of meaning in other phenomena. As Neisser puts it:

> The structures of speech have their own complex rules of formation, which are the proper province of linguistics. Their complexity does not imply, however, that the act of perceiving them is radically different from the way we perceive events of other kinds. (Neisser 1976: 160)

In his model of the perceptual process, Neisser emphasizes the prospective function of schemata (see Discussion 5 in this Chapter):

> In my view, the cognitive structures crucial for vision are the anticipatory schemata that prepare the perceiver to accept certain kinds of information rather than others and thus control the activity of looking. Because we can see only what we know how to look for, it is these schemata (together with the information actually available) that determine what will be perceived. (Neisser 1976: 20)

According to Neisser, the perceiver is directed to explore phenomena by a particular schema. This exploration leads to a sampling of available information, which in turn modifies the schema which activated this 'perceptual cycle' in the first place. This cyclical process is represented diagrammatically as follows:

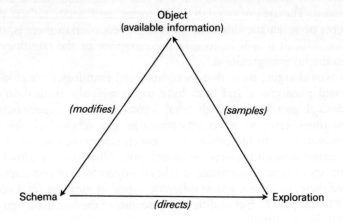

This model of the perceptual cycle bears a close resemblance to Popper's formula for scientific enquiry:

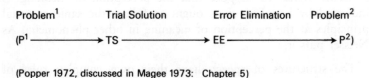

(Popper 1972, discussed in Magee 1973: Chapter 5)

It is easy to see that this could be expressed in the form of Neisser's diagram:

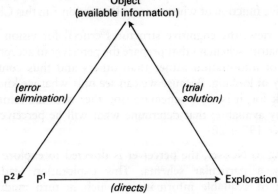

I would suggest, then, that there is reason to suppose that the notion of the schema is crucial to an understanding of how we project perceptual and conceptual order on reality. It must be noted, however, that both Neisser and Popper provide for the adjustment of schemata to account for new experience, so that they direct interpretation, but do not determine it. As Neisser puts it:

> The schema at any given moment resembles a *genotype* rather than a *phenotype*, as these concepts are defined in genetics. It offers a possibility for development along certain lines, but the precise nature of that development is determined only by interaction with an environment. (Neisser 1976: 56)

It is the ability to use linguistic resources to carry out this interaction whereby schematic knowledge is recurrently projected and modified that I refer to as 'capacity'. Because this dynamic interactive process involves both the projection of what is known and a modification of this knowledge in the light of new information, capacity is a principle of both language use and language acquisition.

One might note the relevance here of Piaget's account of learning as involving the complementary processes of *assimilation* and *accommodation* (see Piaget 1953, 1955). Assimilation can be understood as the acceptance of information into established schematic categories, and accommodation as the adjustment of these categories to account for new experience. Capacity, as I use the term, is the ability to maintain the complementary dynamic between these processes in respect to the acquisition and use of language. It is not (as I point out in Discussion 4, Chapter 1) confined to the minds of children but is, as is borne out by Neisser and Popper, an essential requirement for making sense of the world and as crucial to the well-being of the mind as are the processes of respiration and digestion to the body.

8. Frame procedures

In considering procedures for establishing and maintaining frames of reference, we are concerned with how the language user draws on the resources available in the language system to relate different propositions. These resources are exhaustively described in Halliday and Hasan 1976.

We can, of course, take examples of attested language use in the form of transcriptions of spoken interaction and passages of written prose, and note what devices have been used. To do this is to describe the cohesion of texts as formal objects, as products of the discourse process. What I am concerned with here is the discourse process itself, with the procedures which have to be engaged to set up a common frame of reference between interlocutors so that expressions are associated with their required indexical value, and coherence is achieved.

Such a concern is basically ethnomethodological in character, since it looks at discourse from the participant point of view and seeks to enquire into:

> ... the rational properties of practical actions as contingent ongoing accomplishments of organized artful practices of everyday life. (Garfinkel 1972: 321)

> ... the process whereby rules said to cover interactional settings are constructed, as well as with the assessment of claimed measurement of the actual implementation of rules in specific circumstances. Ethnomethodology emphasizes the interpretive work required to recognize that an abstract rule exists which could fit a particular occasion. (Cicourel 1973: 100)

The general basis for procedural work is what Grice has referred to as the 'co-operative principle'. This provides conditions for the negotiation of agreed meaning, both in respect of frames of reference (the concern of this Discussion) and of routines (the concern of the Discussion which follows). Grice identifies four maxims as constitutive of the co-operative principle:

Quantity: Make your contribution as informative as possible. Do not be more informative than required.
Quality: Do not say what you believe to be false. Do not say that for which you lack adequate evidence.
Relation: Be relevant.
Manner: Be perspicuous. Avoid obscurity and ambiguity. Be brief, orderly, and polite.
          (Grice 1975: 45)

The application of this principle to the conveyance of propositional information so that it is schematically organized results in what Clark and Haviland refer to as the 'given-new contract' whereby

> The speaker tries, to the best of his ability, to make the structure of his utterances congruent with his knowledge of the listener's mental world. He agrees to convey information he thinks the listener doesn't yet know as new information. The listener, for

his part, agrees to interpret all utterances in the same light.
(Clark and Haviland 1977: 4)

I take this 'knowledge of the listener's mental world' referred to
here to be ordered (as indicated in Discussion 3 of this chapter) into
ideational schemata, or frames of reference. What the given-new
contract amounts to, therefore, is an agreement between interlocutors that new information should fit into a given frame. Negotiating
this agreement on particular occasions can, however, be a quite
intricate matter.

The problem for the addressee is that he has not only to *identify*
which given information is to be related to an item of new
information, but he has also to *interpret* that relationship in such a
way as to incorporate it into an appropriate frame. In other words,
he needs not only to trace cohesive links between symbols, but must
also achieve coherence by realizing the indexical consequences of
the connection. It is quite possible to identify, for example, the
anaphoric link between a pronoun and an antecedent expression
but still make no sense whatever of the result. Consider the
following:

Statistical probability was discovered in a teapot. A postman saw
it there and connected it to a petrol pump. He was wearing silk
pyjamas at the time. They were old and dusty.

The reader of this somewhat surrealistic piece of prose has no
difficulty identifying *it* as the proform copy of *statistical probability*. The only other possible candidate as antecedent is *teapot*, and
the locative proform *there* which copies the phrase *in the teapot*
eliminates that possibility. Similarly, *he* can be easily related to the
unique antecedent *postman*, and so on. In this case, then, identification does not at all depend on interpretation: having established all
these connections, the reader is still left with nonsense.

Most commonly, however, identification will be impossible
without interpretation, since there will be more than one possible
item of given information which a new item can relate to. In such
cases, the addressee has recourse to various procedures for making
sense. To use a term from Clark and Haviland, he has to 'compute'
the connection. He may do this by inferring a bridge between the
information given and the current state of his knowledge, or by
adding or restructuring the information (see Clark and Haviland
1977: 5–9). The crucial point to make is that these procedures
engage schematic knowledge and seek to establish the indexical

value of the language items concerned. The bridging, adding, and restructuring procedures are directed at assembling the information provided into schematic patterns, and their success in doing this is a measure of the coherence of the discourse. Consider, for example, the following variant on the previous passage:

> Statistical probability was discovered in a teapot. A postman saw it and connected it to a petrol pump. It was old and dusty.

Here there are two possible antecedents for the pronoun *it* in the second sentence, and three in the third. Since there is no recognizable frame of reference, we have no way of taking interpretative bearings on the information, so we cannot identify the proper connection. If we were able to make sense by invoking schematic knowledge, then identification would be possible even when there is no unique antecedent, as for example in the following:

> Statistical probability was discovered in a teapot. A postman was rinsing it out. He had no idea what it was, of course.

We can compute links here between the first *it* and *teapot* and the second *it* and *statistical probability* because we know that teapots are familiar objects, not likely to cause puzzlement in a postman, and get rinsed like other crockery. Interpretation with reference to this knowledge provides the basis for identification.

The point to be stressed, then, is not only that the identification of cohesive links does not of itself lead to a realization of their indexical function, but that it will often depend on the prior recognition of this function. It is only when we see how items converge on a common frame of reference that we make sense of connections and achieve coherence in discourse. The procedures used for inferring relations between propositions (the bridging, adding, restructuring referred to by Clark and Haviland, for example) are essentially *interpretative* procedures as discussed by Cicourel:

> Through the use of interpretive [sic] procedures the participants supply meanings and impute underlying patterns even though the surface content will not reveal these meanings to an observer unless his model is directed to such elaborations.
> (Cicourel 1973: 40)

Cicourel is referring here to spoken discourse. A model that does seek to elaborate meanings so that they do become cohesively explicit is that of Labov and Fanshel 1977, which provides detailed glosses (what they call *expansions*) of spoken interaction so that a discourse which is coherent to the interlocutors but not to the observers is elaborated into a fully cohesive textual variant.

Such elaborations on the part of the observer of spoken discourse derive from the same interpretative procedures that are employed by language users in making sense of language use, whether spoken or written. It is just such procedures ('concept-driven' rather than 'data-driven' as Sanford and Garrod put it (1981: 101)) which enable us to make sense of tautology and metaphor (as discussed in Discussion 6 of this chapter) and which enable Sacks to demonstrate the coherence of the child's story:

The baby cried. The mommy picked it up.

Clark and Haviland offer a similar example:

Horace got some picnic supplies out of the car. The beer was warm.

They comment:

... there is no direct antecedent in the context (i.e. the first) sentence, and so the listener must build a bridge. He must draw the implicature that the picnic supplies contain a quantity of beer, and it is that quantity that is being referred to by the given information of the target (i.e. the second) sentence.
(Clark and Haviland 1977: 21)

In Sacks's terms, *beer* and *picnic supplies* are recognized as belonging to the same 'membership categorization device', that is to say, in my terms, are indexical of the same schematic frame.

It should be noted, too, that it is precisely these interpretative procedures which are engaged in activating the perceptual cycle that Neisser talks about and which constitute what I have called capacity.

It follows from the argument of this Discussion that it is possible to have passages which are impeccably cohesive but nevertheless incoherent in that they are not indexical of frames which represent constructs of familiar or possible worlds. I have already given an example of nonsense of this kind of my own devising. But the nonsense does not have to proclaim itself so overtly. Consider the following:

A. With hocked gems financing him, our hero bravely defied all scornful laughter that tried to prevent his scheme. 'Your eyes deceive', he had said. 'An egg, not a table, correctly typifies this

unexplored planet.' Now three sturdy sisters sought proof.
Forging along, sometimes through calm vastness, yet more
often over turbulent peaks and valleys, days became weeks as
many doubters spread fearful rumours about the edge. At last,
from nowhere, welcome winged creatures appeared, signifying
momentous success. (cited in Dooling and Lachman 1971)

B. The procedure is actually quite simple. First you arrange things
into different groups. Of course, one pile may be sufficient,
depending on how much there is to do. If you have to go
somewhere else due to lack of facilities that is the next step,
otherwise you are pretty well set. It is important not to overdo
things. That is, it is better to do too few things at once than too
many. In the short run this may not seem important, but
complications can easily arise. A mistake can be expensive as
well. At first the whole procedure will seem complicated. Soon,
however, it will become just another facet of life. It is difficult
to see any end to the necessity for this task in the immediate
future, but then one never can tell. After the procedure is
completed, one arranges the materials into different groups
again. Then they can be put into their appropriate places.
Eventually they can be used once more, and the whole cycle
will then have to be repeated. However, that is a part of life.
(cited in Bransford and Johnson 1972)

As they stand, these passages make little if any sense, even though
the symbolic meaning of every term used may be perfectly familiar.
Once a frame is provided, however, in the form of a title, they
become immediately interpretable:

A: Columbus discovers America.
B: Washing clothes.

Our interpretative procedures can now be profitably engaged. In
Passage A, we can realize the indexical meanings to the effect that
the three sisters are Columbus's three ships, that the peaks and
valleys are the waves of the sea, the edge the edge of the world, the
winged creatures birds, and so on. In Passage B, interpretation is a
much simpler matter, since once an indexical value of 'washing
clothes' is provided for the first expression 'procedure', we can
work out the rest by identifying antecedents in a straightforward
way, and little subsequent interpretation is required. In both cases,
however, frame procedures are necessary to work out the propositional meanings that are being indexically signalled.

I have been concerned so far in this Discussion with procedures for establishing a referential connection across elements within a frame. But the connections themselves may be of different kinds. An item of information may contrast with another, or be expressive of time sequence or causality. These relations, (which appear at Level D in the Rhetorical Process Chart in Discussion 3) have been extensively studied in the work of Eugene Winter (see Winter 1971, 1977). This work can be seen as an extension of that of Halliday and Hasan in that it describes the resources within the language system which interpretative procedures operate upon to establish kinds of propositional connectivity.

Winter distinguishes two basic kinds of relation across propositions (he calls them 'clause-relations' but in my terms they are not systemic but schematic phenomena):

> The first is where we match things, actions, people, etc. for same (similar) and different. This is the *Matching Relation*, one of whose characteristic items is *compare*, as in the question, 'How does X compare with Y in respect of Z feature?' and whose replay could be paraphrased as *What is true of X is (not) true of Y*. The second way is where we observe a change in time/space. This is the *Logical Sequence Relation*, whose characteristic lexical items are *connect* and *time* as in the question, 'How does X event connect with Y event (in time)?' ... Included in this sequence is deductive sequence, whose explicit marker is the conjunction *therefore* which signals that the sequence is *premise-conclusion*. (Winter 1977: 6)

These relations are sometimes signalled by so-called 'sentence connectors' (note again Winter's use of systemic terms for schematic function) like *however, thus, therefore, in contrast,* and so on. In my terms, such expressions operate as indices of schematic structure. Indeed, since they are essentially empty of symbolic meaning, one might suggest that their *only* function is indexical, so that they have no place in the systemic description of language, but can be entirely accounted for at the schematic level.

More interestingly, however, Winter points out that these schematic relations can be mediated by 'open class' lexical items which do have independent symbolic meaning. He considers the following example:

> I chose wood rather than aluminium or steel for my structure.

He comments:

The semantic feature which is doing the predicting here is the verb *choose*. The verb is in close association with the reason relation. In discourse structure, there is an inherent predictability when presenting a statement of decision or choice which depends on the following condition. If the reason or basis for the choice has not preceded the statement of choice, then the reason is strongly predicted to follow. (Winter 1977: 3)

It is not, of course, the case that the simple appearance of the lexeme *choose* will always serve as one part of the reason relation. There will be innumerable occasions when its use will call for no provision of a reason at all. It will only do so and realize the indexical meaning Winter associates with it, when the word is used to make a statement which needs to be justified — that is to say, when it expresses a proposition which functions in a certain way in a particular routine. In the example given, the routine in question is that of statement + justification in a student essay.

What Winter describes are various kinds of signal on which interpretative procedures can operate to predict schematic development (see also Hoey 1979). In the case of open class, fully lexical, items like *choose*, he shows how they can be interpreted as indices of propositional relations which are in turn used to realize particular routines (see the comments on the Trimble 'Rhetorical Process Chart' in Discussion 3 in this chapter). But the relations and the realizations must be achieved by procedural interpretation.

9.   Routine procedures

Routine procedures are used to realize how linguistic signs in utterances (spoken or written) are indexical of interpersonal schemata. As with frame procedures, they are derived from the maxims of the general co-operative principle as outlined by Grice.

These procedures are required for the negotiation not of propositional information, but of illocutionary intent, to establish shared knowledge of what kind of communicative act particular utterances are meant to count as when they occur in interaction. Addresser and addressee will assume that utterances will be related to a knowledge of the conditions which define illocutions, both singly and in combination, this knowledge being the interpersonal schemata part of communicative competence. Thus the addresser produces an utterance on the assumption that the addressee will follow the indexical signs and will find warrant for a particular interpersonal interpretation.

Consider, for example, the conditions that define the act of request. These are set down by Labov and Fanshel as follows:

If A addresses to B an imperative specifying an action X at a time T_1, and B believes that A believes that

1a   X should be done (for a purpose Y) (*need for action*)
  b   B would not do X in the absence of the request (*need for the request*)
2   B has the *ability* to do X (with an instrument Z)
3   B has the *obligation* to do X or is willing to do it
4   A has the *right* to tell B to do X
then A is heard as making a valid request for action.
(Labov and Fanshel 1977: 78)

On a particular occasion, an addresser may make reference to one of the conditions set down here in the belief that the others are implicit in the context of utterance. The addressee will therefore have procedural work to do to infer that this particular utterance does indeed relate to this condition. If, for example, the addresser were to say:

I don't have any change

the addressee, subscribing to the co-operative principle, assumes that the addresser is not simply offering irrelevant information, recognizes that the utterance is meant to have a bearing on condition 1a, (i.e. that there is a need, for instance, for the taxi driver to be paid), assumes, further, that the addresser supposes that all other conditions hold, and so interprets the utterance as a request for action (in this case, to pay the fare).

But we must notice that this single act of requesting action is an element in a routine and although it can be analysed in isolation, after the manner of Searle (1969), it functions as a part in interactive structure. Thus a request would normally be followed by a response and the two acts would constitute what Sacks has called an adjacency pair which is, in effect, a simple routine. Coulthard in discussing this makes the following comments:

Sacks observes that a conversation is a string of at least two turns. Some turns are more closely related than others and he isolates a class of sequences of turns called *adjacency pairs* which have the following features: they are two utterances long; the utterances are produced successively by different speakers; the utterances are ordered — the first must belong to the class of *first pair parts*, the second to the class of *second pair parts*; the utterances are related, not any second pair part can follow any first pair part, but only an appropriate one; the first pair part often selects next speaker and always selects next action — it thus sets up a *transition relevance* and expectation which the next speaker fulfils, in other words the first pair of a part predict the occurrence of the second. (Coulthard 1977: 70)

These remarks make the schematic character of these adjacency pairs quite clear.

However, it is not the case that interpersonal schemata always take the form of two-part routines of this kind. If the response to a request is compliant, for example, it will generally be followed by an acknowledgement on the part of the requester, and if not, its absence will be noted, and perhaps give rise to resentment. The following three-part exchange, therefore, would be a normal development from the request considered earlier:

A: I don't have any change.   *Request*
B: Here, let me.   *Compliant response*
A: Oh, thanks.   *Acknowledgement*

The engagement by the interlocutors in this routine, however, obviously depends on the first illocution being recognized as a request, and this is where procedures come in. They may be employed covertly in the form of silent inference and this can be analytically reconstructed as a series of logical steps in the same sort of way as propositional links can be provided by expansion (see Discussion 8 in this chapter). Searle gives an example of such a series of steps representing the procedural work needed to make sense of an indirect request (see Searle 1979 Chapter 2). But the procedures may also be realized as overt negotiation whereby addresser intent and addressee interpretation are brought into alignment. For example:

A: I don't have any change.
B: I don't follow you.
A: We have to pay the taxi and I only have this £10 note.
B: Oh, I see. Here, let me.
A: Thanks.

The first exchange establishes a convergence of intent and interpretation so that the request is achieved and the routine engaged. It is what Jefferson (1972) calls a *side sequence*. In my terms, where such sequences function to establish illocutionary intent, they represent routine procedures; where they clarify propositional information, they represent frame procedures.

Notice that the work of Eugene Winter can be related to the idea of adjacency pairs. The general rhetorical schema that he has proposed (See Discussion 3, this chapter) has such a pair, *problem-solution*, as its central core, with an initial *situation* and a final *evaluation* providing the support elements to make up a four-part routine. The relationships described in the preceding Discussion also can be seen as adjacency pairs in respect of propositional dependencies which define different kinds of frame structure.

10. Formulations

This term comes from Garfinkel and Sacks 1970. The distinction between gist and upshot as types of formulation is made in Heritage and Watson 1979, although they do not relate these phenonema to schemata as I have done. It is, in fact, generally the case that the study of the procedural aspects of discourse carried out by ethnomethodologists has developed independently of the study of its schematic aspects associated with workers in Artificial Intelligence. One of the major tasks of discourse analysis is to achieve a synthesis of the two approaches so that due recognition is given to both the conventional and the creative features of natural language use.

Formulations are the reverse of expansions as discussed in the preceding Discussion. Their function is to reduce propositional and illocutionary elaboration so as to bring the main point (gist or upshot) into prominence. They are used, therefore, as a means of marking progress in the overt negotiation of meaning and are directed at the management of interaction, whether this is spoken or written. But they are also used covertly to reduce information for manageable storage in memory. It is this aspect of formulating that van Dijk refers to when he describes how 'macro-structures' are derived from the whole discourse input by procedures such as generalization, deletion, integration (van Dijk 1977a: 143–8, 1977b). These are conceived of as operations that create mental constructs. It is worth noting that Heritage and Watson (1979) talk about the principal properties of formulations in very similar terms (in their case, preservation, deletion, transformation) but for them formulations take the form of actual utterances which play a part in the development of discourse itself.

The difference between formulations as 'conversational objects', as Heritage and Watson put it, and reductions as cognitive constructs can be traced to the different orientations to discourse study that I referred to earlier. Heritage and Watson are concerned with how information is put in summary form to facilitate interaction, and see the operation, therefore, in procedural terms. Van Dijk is concerned with how such summarizing reduces all the procedural elaboration of a discourse to its underlying schematic structure.

11. Co-operative and territorial imperatives

Grice's co-operative principle (see Discussion 8 in this chapter) relates essentially of course to the co-operative imperative, to accessibility. However, tucked away in the corner of the maxim of manner, reference is made to politeness, and this relates to the territorial imperative in that it has to do with how information is conveyed so that it is acceptable to the addressee.

Acceptability (as I define it here) is discussed in Labov and Fanshel in terms of degrees of mitigation and aggravation (see Labov and Fanshel 1977: 84–6) and given comprehensive treatment in Brown and Levinson 1978. Brown and Levinson use the term 'face' to cover what I have referred to as 'territoriality':

> 'face', the public self-image that every member wants to claim for himself, consisting in two related aspects:
> (a) negative face: the basic claim to territories, personal preserves, rights to non-distraction — i.e. to freedom of action and freedom from imposition
> (b) positive face: the positive consistent self-image or 'personality' (crucially including the desire that this self-image be appreciated and approved of) claimed by interactants.
> (Brown and Levinson 1978: 66)

Utterances which have the effect of intruding into the addressee's life space, the psychic territory he claims as his own and in which he finds his individual security, are 'face-threatening acts', and it is generally in the interests of both interlocutors that they should be mitigated in some way. Brown and Levinson propose a number of procedures for this purpose, which they call 'strategies'. Among them are:

> Notice, attend to H(earer). (His interests, wants, needs, goods)
> Exaggerate (interest, approval, sympathy with H)
> Intensify interest to H

Use in-group identity markers
Seek agreement
Avoid disagreement
etc.

It will be clear that these procedures for mitigating the possible face-threatening force of an utterance to make it more acceptable will frequently run counter to procedures designed to make the intent of the addresser more immediately accessible.

Notice that although I have set the co-operative and territorial imperatives in opposition, the mutual recognition of territorial rights and of the need to protect face is a co-operative contract of a kind, which is why politeness appears in the small print, as it were, in one of the Gricean maxims. Lakoff would appear to regard what I have called accessibility and acceptability as of equal weight, since she proposes that the co-operative principle (in a general sense) can be reduced to two maxims: 1. Be clear (i.e. accessible) 2. Be polite (i.e. acceptable) (see Lakoff 1973).

Wilson and Sperber, on the other hand, identify relevance as the salient maxim and so focus attention on the accessibility factor (see Smith and Wilson 1979 Chapter 8, Wilson and Sperber 1981), and Leech, in stressing the importance of tact, focuses attention on acceptability (Leech 1977).

3   Course design and methodology

A   Argument

In Chapter 1, I suggested that ESP courses might be ranged on a scale of decreasing specificity, with those at the most specific end being concerned essentially with training and those at the less specific end, which shades into general purpose English (GPE), essentially concerned with education. Training was defined as a course of instruction directed at the solution of problems established in advance and amenable to the application of formulae of a relatively fixed and restricted kind. The effectiveness of training depends on narrowing the gap between formula and problem. Education, on the other hand, was defined as a course of instruction which prepared people to cope with problems not specified in advance and not therefore to be accounted for by simply correlating them with known formulae. The effectiveness of education, therefore, depends on developing the capacity to interpret formula and problem in such a way as to bridge the gap between them.

We can now express these distinctions by reference to the model of language use developed in the preceding chapter. Language training, we may say, sets out to provide a knowledge of a restricted set of schemata, those frames of reference and rhetorical routines which characterize a particular area of language use. The objectives of a course of training will be directed at achieving just this aim, and any procedural capacity which develops which will allow the learner to go beyond the specified aim can be regarded as a contingent benefit. Of course, to the extent that all training, even the most narrowly constrained, must allow for some room for manoeuvre, some lack of fit between formula and problem, there will be some need for procedural activity. But the more specific the training is, the more it will be focused on the required schemata.

Educational objectives have to be defined in procedural terms, since there is no clear set of schemata in immediate prospect. What an educational course will seek to do is to develop a procedural capacity which will enable the learner to deal with a range of different frames of reference and rhetorical routines as occasion requires in the future and after completion of the course. It is possible to shift along the specificity scale and take bearings on likely aims, allowing these to indicate a more schematic definition of objectives.

If we were to operate at the extreme ends of this scale, we would design courses on the one hand with reference only to schemata without regard to procedures, and on the other hand courses with reference to procedures without regard to schemata. In practice, courses reveal different emphases rather than exclusive focus. We would expect to find, for example, that what have been referred to as 'narrow angle' ESP courses, with titles like 'English for Mechanical Engineers', 'English for Bank Cashiers', do tend towards a schematic approach to course design, whereas so-called 'wide angle' courses would tend towards a procedural approach, their purpose being to focus attention on study skills rather than on a particular area of use to which they would apply.

Notice, however, that when I talk about these tendencies, I am referring to the objectives that the course design is intended to satisfy, not to the means for implementing them. So a course which is directed at schematic objectives may well include procedural activities as a methodological means to that end, and conversely, a procedure-oriented course may well use schematic exercises of one sort or another. Indeed it is hard to see how either kind of course could actually be implemented otherwise. Similarly, a course might introduce exercises pitched at what I have called in the preceding chapter the systemic level of linguistic knowledge — exercises, for example, in sentence composition. These too would usually be justified as a methodological means to an end, not as an end in themselves.

The difference, and the relationship, between ends and means is not, it would seem, always very clearly understood. When it is proposed, for example, that language courses should adopt a communicative approach to presentation, whereby structures are given a notional and functional realization, many teachers claim that this is the approach they already practise. They point to the use of dialogues in different social settings — the theatre, the restaurant, the railway station — and say that they are by this means representing, indeed getting learners to participate in, actual language use. Now these dialogues can be seen as schemata: they illustrate certain scenarios, frames of reference linked to rhetorical routines. But if they are used simply to display aspects of the linguistic system, as they very commonly are, they are not *realized* as schemata. The only way they could be realized is, as I have argued in the preceding chapter, by procedural activity, and there is usually very little evidence of that. Generally learners are required to note how the dialogue manifests formal items: it is not re-presented as a problem to be solved by having interpretative procedures engage the appropriate schema. So these instances of so-called situational presentation have the appearance but not the reality of schemata because they are associated not with procedures but with linguistic structures. They are used as a means towards imparting linguistic competence.

There is a similar confusion between kinds of comprehension question. With reference to the three levels of language knowledge and ability distinguished in the preceding chapter, some questions are systemic, some schematic, and some procedural, and it is seldom clear how they are meant to relate, and which are intended to be simply facilitating as means to the acquisition of ability represented by the others. I have discussed comprehension question types elsewhere and have made the distinction between reference, assimilation, and discrimination questions. Reference questions, which call for the demonstration of linguistic competence, are, in terms of the model of language use I have developed here, systemic in character. Assimilation questions are procedural and call for the recovery of implied meaning so as to establish frames of reference and routines. And discrimination questions, which call for a summary in respect of gist or upshot, are schematic. It would seem to make sense to use these different types of question in such a way as to make clear what the dependency is between them. If their purpose is to develop communicative capacity, then presumably procedural questions have priority and the other types are justi-fiable only because they play a supporting role, with systemic questions perhaps establishing a linguistic base where necessary and schematic questions drawing attention to the consequences of the effective use of procedures. (**B** 1)

ESP has been no more explicit than has GPE about the way means and ends might be related. Indeed the assumption seems often to be that there is no necessary relationship between them at all. We noted in the last chapter, for example, that Munby devises an instrument for syllabus design in complete detachment from any methodological question of how it might be effectively imple-mented. The specificity of ESP refers to the aims of learning and not to the activities that need to be engaged in to bring these aims about. In general, the belief appears to be that there is nothing specific about the learning *process* of ESP students, but only about the *product* of their learning.

If this is so, then does this mean that when aims are dissociated from objectives, which then have to be pedagogically defined, and a course in consequence becomes more educationally oriented, that it moves abruptly out of the ESP field and into GPE? For the logic of the situation would seem to require this conclusion. Consider the matter. When objectives are not a direct reflex of aims, that is to say when the learning product is not exactly specifiable, then they have to be defined in such a way as to develop a *process* in the learner *towards* his eventual aim. They have to be based, therefore, on some description of learning, not what has to be learned. So in outlining objectives, we have to take methodological means into account.

So long as we conceive of ESP as simply a matter of analysing learners' needs in respect of their aims in learning, thereby avoiding the problem of devising objectives and a methodology to fulfil them, then it is a very straightforward affair. It is also invalid as a pedagogic enterprise. It assumes that all ESP is training of a most rigid and inflexible sort which fashions human resources into a shape which will fit into the slot of manpower needs. If the only thing we can be specific about is a set of aims, then ESP has no pedagogic significance at all, as far as I can see. It becomes no more than an administrative convenience.

The only justification for ESP, as a separate area of enquiry and practice, lies, it seems to me, in establishing principles for describing its objectives, as I have defined them in this book. And in the rest of this chapter my purpose is to attempt to do that in the light of the model of language use I have previously outlined.

Let us begin by supposing that we are required to design a course of English for students who need the language to read their specialist textbooks. How might we proceed? One way would be to get hold of the textbooks they have to read and carry out a linguistic analysis to establish the defining characteristics of this particular register. Such a characterization would be essentially quantitative in that it would indicate which lexical items and syntactic structures occurred most frequently in the data. It would in this sense be a systemic description of aims, a representation of the linguistic forms that the students are most likely to encounter and be obliged to interpret in their reading. The result would be a collection of component parts. The next step might be to equate aims and objectives by assuming that since the students' aim is to use these components, then the objective of the course should simply be to teach them.

The difficulty that arises here is that these linguistic units become components of discourse only when they occur in the context of language use. To identify something as a component is to recognize the operational complex as a whole in which it functions as a part. If analysis isolates elements from this complex, then it must deny them the functional features which alone can give them their component status. To the extent that register analysis involves, as it commonly does, the isolation of formal linguistic types from contexts of use, then it cannot account for their function as components of discourse. What it does instead is to express these elements as components functioning within the formal linguistic system. So what this kind of analysis does, in effect, is to impose on the schematic and procedural activity of language use categories of description appropriate only to the systemic level of linguistic organization. It therefore converts elements of language from one kind of component, where it functions as a part of discourse, to another kind, where it functions as a part of the linguistic system.

So such an analysis will not of itself tell us, for example, how the frequency of certain types of lexis and syntactic structure provides evidence for commonly occurring schemata in the textbooks under consideration. It will tell us that certain lexical items are very common, but it will not tell us how they relate in defining particular frames of reference. It will tell us that certain syntactic structures are especially favoured, but it will not tell us how they are used in the realization of types of rhetorical routine which characterize the kind of discourse concerned. There will be no clear indication either about which linguistic elements are essentially procedural in func-tion. It has been pointed out, for example, that apart from the specialist vocabulary of certain areas of use which provide the basis for identifying register, there is also present in any corpus of language a wide range of so-called 'common-core' words which have no such restriction on use. In the terms of the model I am developing here, specialist lexis serves to define particular frames of reference and has, therefore, a schematic role to play, whereas common-core vocabulary serves the general procedural purpose of realizing these particular schemata. (B 2)

The limitations of the approach I have been outlining here to the specification of aims become particularly apparent when one considers how its findings might be implemented in course design.

The purpose of such a course must be to prepare the students to process the written discourse of their textbooks and this means that they will have somehow to be guided towards using the linguistic elements extracted by analysis as discourse components. But the analysis has produced only components of the linguistic system, so the only way of achieving these objectives must be to devise a pedagogy which re-instates these elements at the level of use, and so converts them back into what they were before they were subjected to analysis. But such conversion can be carried out only if it is known how these elements function in the particular area of use we are concerned with, and it is precisely this kind of information which a formal analysis fails to provide. So what is to be done? One might, of course, simply teach these formal items in association with topics taken from the target textbooks and just hope for the best, leaving the learner to find his own way towards communicative realization. To do this is to adopt a conventional GPE approach, and to assume that specific purposes are not to be incorporated into pedagogic objectives at all. The use of specific *topics* to serve as a vehicle for formal items simply becomes a device, perhaps useful for motivation (of which more later), for giving some face validity to the teaching of linguistic competence.

Alternatively, one might strike out in a different direction and look for ways of defining the aims of our students in communicative terms by devising a means of analysis which preserved the essential discourse features of language use instead of analysing them out of existence. It might appear on the face of it that this requirement is met by the descriptive device proposed by Munby. What, then, do the specific purposes of these students look like when this particular instrument is used for their analysis?

Perhaps the first point that needs to be made is that this device is directed at describing features of the communicative process, and linguistic forms are thus seen as a realization of this process and not as the manifested tokens of the language system. It is concerned, therefore, with aspects of discourse and not, as is the case with the kind of register analysis I have just reviewed, simply with their textual reflex. So the device is constructed out of sociolinguistic concepts. But it is important to note that it is indeed a device and nothing more, put together by using whatever theory seems serviceable and directed towards a practical outcome. It is not a model if we mean by that the representation of a coherent theory of language. It is to be assessed, therefore, by how effectively it achieves its declared purpose of defining the content of purpose-specific language programmes.

What emerges, then, from an application of this device, and how far is it a satisfactory definition of what the content of an ESP course should be?

The device carries out two operations: the first produces a profile of needs by reference to factors in the communicative events that the learner will have eventually to be involved in, and the second then interprets these needs in terms of three kinds of element, each representing a different aspect of language behaviour. Thus the first part deals with features of the situation that learners will encounter, and the second part with features of communicative activity they will have to engage in to cope effectively with the situation. The three kinds of behavioural element in this communicative activity are called language skills, functions, and forms. A direct correlation of language forms with situational factors would, of course, yield findings of the sort associated with register analysis, as already discussed in this chapter. The Munby device, however, has these two other kinds of element (skills and functions) mediating between the situational factors and linguistic forms, and the latter are brought into the picture only as realizations of these other elements.

There are, however, a number of issues which arise about the nature of the mediation and of the elements that are supposed to effect it. We may begin with a consideration of language skills. These are presented as a long list of operations which are presupposed by the general ability to process discourse, ranging from phonological discrimination to the tracing of propositional cross-reference. But these operations are arranged in sets under various sub-heads, with no indication at all of how they inter-relate in actual language use. Thus, for example, we have a skill which is called 'understanding relations between parts of a text through lexical cohesion', which is sub-divided into seven types, and a different skill called 'understanding relations between parts of a text through grammatical cohesion', which is divided into six types. Here, then, we have two distinct sets of features abstracted out of actual behaviour. In language use, these skills, these areas of know-how, are exploited in all kinds of different ways and combine with all kinds of other skills appearing in this list under separate headings. But we are given no clue at all as to how this complex exploitation actually takes place. What we have here, in fact, is an atomistic analysis of *procedures* which reduces them to a set of static features. (See Discussion 2, Chapter 2.)

The same sort of prismatic operation is applied to the second of the behavioural elements that are dealt with in this device. In the case of language skills, we have an itemization of various features of interpretative procedures, their dynamic and creative character reduced to a static inventory of parts. In the case of language functions, we have an itemization of various features of *schemata*, but similarly fragmented. In both cases we have a description of *parts*, procedural parts on the one hand and schematic parts on the other. What is missing, and what this kind of operation of its nature cannot provide, is the means of characterizing how these parts are activated and related in the actual discourse process. The device itself is a processor, but its analytic operations no more represent the process of language use than do those of a generative grammar.

The kinds of analysis I have been considering are of necessity concerned with categories of competence, with the knowledge that is *presupposed* by the effective use of language. What they do not deal with, and cannot of their nature deal with, is the realization of this knowledge as actual communicative behaviour. They do not tell us what the language user does with the knowledge that has been so neatly itemized, nor, by the same token, how the language learner acquires this knowledge.

This is no criticism of the analyses as such, but of the pedagogic claims that are made for them. All analysis is based on idealization of primary data and seeks to separate elements out from the complexity of their natural surroundings so that they can be ordered into rational arrangements (see Discussion 1, Chapter 2). But these arrangements do not represent the actuality of behaviour: they are constructs of its constituent parts. For the language user to act upon the knowledge that has been so itemized, he has to put the idealization process into reverse. Language behaviour is not a reflex of competence, a simple projection of systems and schemata, but a realization of competence through procedural activity, which creates the primary data of language use. If we are to make our language learners into language users, we have to devise ways, therefore, of engaging them in procedural work which will convert these items of knowledge into actualized communicative behaviour. We need a methodology to activate these inert categories.

But methodology has been generally neglected in ESP. The emphasis has been on *what* ought to be taught, on content, rather than on *how* it should be taught. Courses have been designed to incorporate the systemic and schematic features of particular areas of language use, rather than the activities that users in these areas characteristically engage in to achieve a procedural realization of these features in the discourse process. Hence there is commonly a disparity between the specificity of content in ESP textbooks and the conventional language teaching methodology which takes no account of the specific kinds of activity which learners are engaged in within their academic and occupational fields. The assumption behind this is that what learners need is a knowledge of the systemic and schematic features of the English of their speciality, and that this can be conveyed to them by conventional means of a very general sort, which need have no connection at all with the activities for which they need to use English. Any methodology will do so long as it gets the information across. So it is that students of science and technology are often required to read off structures from a substitution table, fill in the blanks, transform one sentence into another and so on without regard to whether these somewhat mechanistic operations are in any way congruent with the kind of intellectual activity required of these students in the pursuit of their specialist studies. Since they are learning English to further these studies, one might expect that the congruence ought to be considerable, that the specificity of ESP ought to apply to learning activity as well as the knowledge to be learned, and therefore to methodology as well as to content. The emphasis, however, has been on making content specific. The assumption has generally been that we already have a well-tried language-teaching methodology to hand and that this will serve the purpose, whether specific or not. I believe this view to be mistaken. (**B** 3)

   This belief follows naturally from the model of language use proposed in the preceding chapter. The schemata which represent different combinations of concepts (or frames of reference) and different ways of communicating (or rhetorical routines) can, as we have seen, be analysed into their constituent elements, and this yields functional or notional component items, analogous to structural items derived from the language system, idealized out of context and in consequence deprived of their essential force as features of language use. This force can be restored only by reversing the idealization process through the application of procedures for making sense. These procedures can, in turn, be activated only by a methodology which engages the learner in activities which he would normally engage in when putting language to use for particular purposes. Without such procedures, neither systemic nor schematic knowledge is realized, so there is no discourse, no language use, but only display of language usage as sentence or text.

These procedures, however, do not operate on isolated items, but on larger schematic units. Just as schemata cannot be realized without procedures, so procedures have no point unless they are schematically orientated. The meaningful use of language, therefore, also requires that procedural activities should be purposefully directed towards realization of schemata of some sort which learners will accept as having some connection with their own concerns. This is where course design comes in.

But on what principle are the elements of course content to be ordered into a design? The kind of analytic itemization favoured by needs analysis of the kind previously considered does not provide one. It provides only a list of component parts. It seems clear that course design must in some way be a projection of 'macro-units', that is to say the frames of reference or routines which are associated with recognizable 'speech events' or schematic types, conventional patterns of language use. (**B 4**)

Such patterns may be evident in the way particular frames of reference are linked with particular routines, and in this case they provide a basis for the design of 'narrow angle' ESP courses. As was pointed out earlier in this chapter, where such courses place the emphasis on the schematic knowledge, i.e. the competence to be acquired, they would be located at the more specific end of the spectrum and accordingly be more training-orientated. It should be noted, however, that such courses will have an educational dimension to the extent that course design based on such specific schemata will be implemented through procedural work. Except in extreme cases where fixed formulae are learnt by rote, schemata cannot otherwise be realized and therefore the required competence cannot otherwise be acquired. The activity of realization will itself develop the capacity for further use and learning beyond that which is incorporated in course design. It is for this reason that it is so important that methodology should be concerned with appropriate procedural activity.

Courses of the 'wide angle' kind still need to draw on schematic patterns for their design, even though they are more procedure-orientated in their intent. But in this case, the patterns are of an underlying sort, a set of general frames of reference and routines which, it is assumed, inform a range of topical areas of use and which can therefore be realized in pedagogic terms by a variety of different topics. Here, as a matter of principle, topics are selected for their effectiveness in implementing the objectives of the course without regard to their immediate relevance to eventual aims. It is also possible for 'narrow angle' courses to justify their specific topics on methodological grounds, as we shall see presently, but in the case of 'wide angle' courses such a criterion for selection is a matter of principle.

Whether a relatively wide or narrow angle approach to ESP course design is preferred will depend on a number of factors. There may, for example, be purposes, most likely relating to occupational and technical training, which can be more effectively serviced by greater specificity of schematic design; or the choice may be constrained by considerations like face validity or apparent cost effectiveness. Other purposes will call for a more educational, less specific approach. It would be a mistake to insist on the inherent superiority of one approach, or indeed to think of them as necessarily at odds with each other. What must however be insisted upon, it seems to me, is the importance of recognizing that the effectiveness of an approach, wherever it may be located on the specificity spectrum, depends on establishing a principled relationship between course design and methodology. The shift towards specificity will generally mean that purpose is conceived of as the acquiring of a limited competence, and the schematic content of the course will then approximate more closely to the language of eventual aims. But there will still be the necessity of establishing pedagogic objectives. This means the devising of a methodology to involve the learners in appropriate procedural activities which will enable them to engage their capacity and realize the schematic content of the course to achieve the competence they need and the ability to exploit it subsequently in actual instances of language use. No matter how schematically specific a course may be, no matter how fixedly orientated towards aims, it will normally require a procedurally based methodology, for otherwise the learner is given no experience of natural language and therefore no real provision for the achievement of his purpose, specific or otherwise.

With wide angle course design, the need to account for the procedural aspect of learning and use is more self evident. Here, the intention is obviously not to get students to internalize the topical realizations, but to use them for learning. It is the process of relating these particular realizations to more general schematic structures which is the central concern and the process must, as is evident from the argument in Chapter 2, involve procedural activity. There is less emphasis here on specific competence and more on general capacity. This means that pedagogic objectives cannot but be considered as distinct from aims and so there is less likelihood of their being confused.

But equally, of course, there is less likelihood of the objectives being recognized as relevant by the learner. This is the problem of face validity. Students of engineering, for example, may reject the idea that they can develop their capability in the language they need for their specialized studies by dealing with topics like the structure of the atom or the life cycle of the frog, and if we cannot engage their interest we will not engage their learning. This is not only a matter of motivation. As I pointed out earlier in this chapter, if learners see no reason for achieving meaning in respect of particular activities, they will not engage procedures and so cannot authenticate the language as discourse at all. The language learners' interest is an intrinsic part of the language using process itself, not a state of mind it is desirable for learners to be in so as to make them more receptive to teaching.

The challenge for the wide angle approach to ESP, then, is to ensure that topics that have no direct bearing on aims are selected and presented in such a way that, despite their lack of specificity, they will activate the capacity for language use and learning. The most obvious way of doing this is to represent these topics as problems calling for the same kind of thinking for their solution, the same type of procedural work as learners would be required to use in their field of specialization. (B 5)

We are again drawn back to the central importance of methodology. The argument I have been following in this book leads (logically it seems to me) to the conclusion that sound ESP pedagogy requires that course design should service methodology and not, as seems to be the prevalent view, the other way round. It does not actually matter very much, I think, what language the learners are presented with. What does matter is how they can put it to effective use. Even in the case of the more narrow angle course, the more cogent reason for specificity is not that the language corresponds to aims, but that it is more likely to be realized as meaningful by the learners. By the same token, it does not much matter that a course does not provide comprehensive coverage of what has eventually to be learnt — even if this were possible. What does matter is that what is included should activate learning, so that provision is made for the learners to achieve their own aims after the course is over by applying the procedures they have used in learning to the continuation of learning through language use.

B   Discussion

1.   *Comprehension questions*

The discussion of types of comprehension question referred to here appears in Widdowson 1978 Chapter 3.

Notice that the difference in function of these questions may influence the decision as to where they are actually to be positioned. If they are of a procedural kind, they figure in the process of immediate interpretation, and it would seem to make sense, therefore, to have them appear as a continuing accompaniment to the passage. This was the reasoning behind the insertion of comprehension checks in the reading passages of the *English in Focus* series. However, this device has the disadvantage of requiring the learner to refer back to the previous reading of a paragraph after the event, an activity clearly more appropriate for schematic operations. Perhaps a more satisfactory format for procedural questions is that adopted in *Reading and Thinking in English*, where the reader is prompted from the margin.

Whereas procedural questions aim at drawing the reader's attention to the interactive process of discourse in flight, as it were, schematic questions are directed at the formulations of gist and upshot (see Discussion 10 in Chapter 2), that is to say, the summary extrapolation of salient information. Such questions, therefore, are logically placed at the end of paragraphs or of the passage as a whole.

2.   *Procedural vocabulary*

The notion of a 'common core' vocabulary has a long history. In the extensive work carried out on word counts, which culminated in West's *General Service List of English Words* (West 1953), it was found that certain lexical items of high aggregate frequency also occurred across a wide range of texts. It follows that these 'common core' items are not schematically bound, and in consequence are subject to a wide range of interpretation. In other words, they have high indexical potential or valency, and this is in inverse proportion to their degree of symbolic specificity. The item *do*, for example, used as a general stand-in for a fully lexical verb (a pro-verb) has the potential to refer to any activity, and accordingly is almost entirely lacking in specificity as a symbol, which is why it can also be used as a dummy carrier of tense and negation. An item like *dote*, on the other hand, is symbolically highly specific and can be indexical in use to a relatively narrow range of reference; and where we have such a narrow range that the item is bound to a fixed collocation, like *addled* or *rancid*, the indexical meaning is directly derivable from the symbolic, and the range reduces to zero. In general, then, we may state it as a rule that the greater the lexical content of a word, the more narrow its indexical range: lexicality is in inverse proportion to indexicality.

It follows from this that words of wide indexical range are especially useful for negotiating the conveyance of more specific concepts, for defining terms which relate to particular frames of reference. That is to say, such words function as a *procedural* vocabulary for establishing the terms which characterize different schemata and which are used to identify 'registers' (see Discussion 5 in Chapter 1). Consider the following entries in the *Oxford Advanced Learner's Dictionary of Current English*:

> *pinnate* (bot) (of a leaf) formed of small leaves on opposite sides of a stem
> *pipette* slender tube for transferring small quantities of liquid, esp in chemistry.

The terms *pinnate* and *pipette* are specifically indexical of the schematic frames of reference of botany and chemistry. They are defined by the use of 'common core' or procedural words. And in particular contexts of use, they would be explained or demonstrated by such words. This is the essential point behind the observations made by Hutchinson and Waters about everyday language in technical communication:

> The language used in technical education is not, except for a few examples of terminology, subject specific nor even specific to technical communication. Everyday language is used.
> (Hutchinson and Waters 1980a: 3)

What Hutchinson and Waters are referring to here is the language used procedurally for technical explanation and demonstration (see also Hutchinson and Waters 1980b, 1981). Ewer, who takes them to task on this point, expresses his objection in the following way:

> ... I find it difficult to believe that Hutchinson and Waters are intending to imply (as they are) that there is no essential difference between the language predominantly used by a hotel receptionist, that of a telex from a business firm, a manual of technical instructions or a paper read at a scientific meeting.
> (Ewer 1981: 7)

The word 'predominantly' is critical here. If predominance is to be measured by frequency of occurrence, then Hutchinson and Waters are surely correct: there will be more words, as formal items, which the three areas of use cited by Ewer will have in common than there will be words which differentiate them. Of course, most of these items will be so-called 'function words': articles, particles, auxiliary verbs, prepositions. But there is no hard and fast division between such words and fully blown lexemes, only degrees of lexical content. This is why, as I mentioned earlier, words which have independent lexical status but are of high indexical valency slip easily into syntactic functions. *Do, make, go* are examples which spring immediately to mind. Indeed, syntactic function might be defined as the reduction of lexical content in the interests of increased indexical flexibility.

If, however, predominance means what is schematically distinctive, then of course Ewer is right: there will be terms marking the discourse of receptionists which differ from those marking the discourse of technical instructions. But these will be the less frequent words of narrow range, since they would not otherwise be distinctive.

It seems clear that Hutchinson and Waters are thinking of the *procedural* vocabulary which is used in instruction and are focusing attention on the process of learning, whereas Ewer is thinking of the *schematic* vocabulary which defines and makes distinctive particular frames of reference in different areas of use. This suggests that Hutchinson and Waters are more concerned with questions of methodology, with the kind of activity that promotes the learning of language, with *how* students *learn*, whereas Ewer is more concerned with what has to be put into a course as representing the language of the students' eventual aim, with *what* is to be *taught*. I discuss in more detail what I understand to be Ewer's position in the Discussion that follows.

Meanwhile, it is perhaps worth nothing that the problems of procedural and schematic vocabulary are acknowledged, by implication, in the use made of the findings of word counts in the design of structural syllabuses. The criteria of frequency and range indicate the indexical value of a word, but they cannot be used exclusively for determining what is to be taught, quite simply because words of high indexical valency are relatively empty of lexical content: they are auxiliary, enabling devices. There has to be something that they are indexical *of*, there has to be some *schematic* content to the syllabus. This was provided by the invoking of another criterion, that of *teachability*, which makes provision for the use of terms like *book, pen, pencil, chalk, blackboard*, all of which are associated with the classroom frame of reference. *Teachability* was, in effect, a schematic consideration, necessary for the proper function of the procedural vocabulary established by the criteria of frequency and range. One might suggest that the advantage of ESP is that it provides ready-made schemata for the procedural vocabulary to get to grips with.

3. Methodology

The idea that methodology in ESP has been neglected in favour of a concentration on content runs directly counter to views recently expressed in a paper written by J. R. Ewer and O. Boys (Ewer and Boys 1981). Since Ewer was one of the early workers in this field and can claim authority from long experience, and since the paper appeared in the new *ESP Journal*, which is likely to circulate widely among ESP practitioners, it seems important to consider with some care the points that the paper raises, so that we can be clear about the issues involved.*

The paper passes under review a representative set of ESP textbooks published over the past ten years and reveals them to be seriously deficient with reference to the authors' particular criteria for evaluation. The central criterion is the extent to which a textbook's content corresponds with the set of 65 'microacts', or 'communicative operations' (essentially, it would seem, notional/ functional categories) which are said to characterize formal scientific discourse. The argument is that if a textbook does not contain these 'microacts', together with a thorough exemplification of how they are formally realized in English, then it will be defective as a means of preparing students to cope with this kind of discourse.

Content, then, is defined in terms of schematic, rather than systemic, elements; that is to say, in terms of notional/functional categories of the Council of Europe kind. In this respect, the authors of the paper subscribe to the kind of specification of items laid down by Munby and referred to in the previous chapter

---

*Just after writing this Discussion, I learned of the sad death of Jack Ewer. This seems a suitable place to pay tribute to his pioneer work in the field of ESP. Although we differed in our views, I recognize the value of his achievement. The comments I make here are offered in the spirit of scholarship that Jack Ewer himself was always anxious to promote. In this sense, though they are critical, they are also commemorative.

(although Munby is not mentioned). This is clear from the following quotation:

> Content, i.e. the kind of language-in-action taught, is therefore of
> fundamental importance and needs to be determined with as
> much precision and detail as possible. (Ewer & Boys 1981: 96)

Munby's device is designed expressly to determine 'the content of
purpose-specific language programmes'.

The shift from the structural elements of the language system to
the notional/functional elements of schemata in the definition of
content is a departure from the principles which informed the
design of the textbook *A Course in Basic Scientific English*, of
which Ewer himself was joint author (Ewer and Latorre 1969). In
the introduction to this textbook we are told that the 'basic
language of scientific English ... is made up of sentence patterns,
structural (functional) words and non-structural vocabulary ...'
(p. ix). This content has also been determined by extensive research,
'a scrutiny of more than three million words of modern scientific
English'. In other words, the content is derived from a register
analysis. Now this textbook is among those which are shown to be
deficient with reference to the new unit of analysis, the 'microact'.

> The percentage of significant microacts dealt with in the text-
> books ranged from a mere 14% of the total to a still very
> deficient 43% .... (Ewer & Boys 1981: 91)

It would appear, then, by this testimony, that the register analysis
previously conducted was an inadequate device for determining
content. So the evidence would seem to support my own reservations about the efficacy of such analysis. The authors of the paper
quote a statement in which I express these reservations and dismiss
it as a 'partial and misleading exegesis' (p. 99). But their own
evidence would seem to substantiate my view. Otherwise there is no
point in undertaking another extensive analysis by reference to
'microacts'.

Of course, this shift towards a notional approach to the definition of course content does not of itself invalidate the previous
approach, nor does it necessarily lend support to my own view on
register analysis. Everything depends on the validity of the 'microact' as a unit of discourse analysis. We are told that it is a 'basic
unit of communicative intention (corresponding roughly to the
Council of Europe's "functions" and "notions")' (p. 91). This rather
vague formulation makes it difficult to assess the validity of the

criticism which is levelled against the ten textbooks that are arraigned for judgement in this paper, because there is really no way of assessing the evidence. The figures of 14%, 43%, and so on as percentages of 'significant microacts' are meaningless unless we know what the microacts are, and how their significance has been established. The authors are insistent on the need for precision in the specification of content but are not very precise about the concept upon which such specification crucially depends. And no examples are given to help us.

What, then, can these 'microacts' be? They apparently have some rough resemblance to notions and functions, and are variously referred to as 'communicative operations', 'units of communicative intention', 'language-in-action' and 'language and language-related factors in comprehension and prediction in formal scientific discourse'. We may conclude from this that these microacts are schematic elements; notional items which combine in frames of reference which define the conceptual content of science, and functional items which combine to create the routines which are most commonly used in scientific communication. The very prefix 'micro' indicates that these are constituents of larger discourse units which analysis has isolated as separate items.

This brings us again to the question that was raised in connection with the Munby device: how is a knowledge of these constituents used in the actual discourse process? We do not communicate by issuing tokens of microacts, by simply projecting the categories of our knowledge. We do so by means of the procedural activity of making sense whereby conventional schemata are realized, modified, extended so that shared knowledge is achieved. Unless this procedural activity is engaged, no communication takes place, no discourse occurs. It seems clear, therefore, that a central task for teaching is to set up conditions whereby learners will actually engage these discourse procedures to achieve what they can recognize as relevant communicative outcomes. If they do not use their knowledge as a resource in this way, they will not be operating at a discourse level at all. This is where methodology comes in: its function is to devise activities which will promote the use of procedures for making sense.

There are instances in existing textbooks of methodology put to this purpose. The first title in the 'Focus' series, *English in Physical Science*, for example, was used deliberately by its authors to explore the possibility of appropriate methodology of this kind, a methodology which would make appeal to the specific concerns and intellectual dispositions of learners. Hence the comprehension checks inserted in the reading passage and their related solutions; hence the information transfer exercises, which were designed not as language problems but as problems which called for the use of language to solve them. It is not fair to dismiss these exercises as 'methodological gimmickry'. Although they had their imperfections, they were, I think, a matter of how the design principle was put into practice, not of the principle itself. This principle was based on the implicit recognition of the importance of procedural activity. The *Focus* series has been criticized on the grounds that the coverage of the schematic elements of particular areas of enquiry lacks comprehensiveness and consistency (e.g. Coulthard 1977: 148–53). There is some truth in that charge, and the books are deficient in this respect. But the main purpose was not to seek schematic coverage, as it is with Ewer and Boys, but to use what seemed to be salient schematic features to activate interpretative procedures. The focus, therefore, was on the objectives of appropriate methodology.

It is important to be clear about the point at issue here. What Ewer and Boys are saying is that the central consideration in ESP course design is significant content, defined as the extent to which the number of notional/functional items dealt with correspond with their occurrence in the kind of language associated with the specific area of use concerned. *How* they are dealt with is not seen as an ESP matter. The methodology can be, indeed ought to be, that of conventional general purpose language teaching. Attempts to make methodology specific seem to be regarded as a misplaced indulgence in ingenuity to conceal the fundamental deficiency of content. All that is needed is 'the basic methodological apparatus of explanations, examples and exercises' (Ewer and Boys 1981: 95).

Although the textbooks under review are criticized for failing to use this basic apparatus, we are not actually given any indication of how it would in fact operate on the microacts that constitute course content, referred to as 'teaching points' (not, it might be significant to note, as *learning* points). But Ewer's earlier work, *A Course in Basic Scientific English*, might afford us some clue as to what is intended. Indeed, by the authors' own argument, basic methodology should not be affected by any change in the manner of defining content, so this textbook ought to serve as a fairly reliable guide.

Unit I of this textbook deals with the Simple Present Tense. After the presentation of a reading passage (about which, more presently), an explanation is provided about the use of this tense in general. But no guidance is given to the student for distinguishing between the use of this tense 'for stating general truths' and its use 'for describing processes in a general way'. The expression 'Science plays an important role in the societies in which we live' is said to be the expression of a general truth, whereas 'A scientist observes carefully . . .' is said to be the general description of a process; but the students are left to work out the difference between these expressions for themselves. Such an explanation hardly provides a clear conceptual guide upon which the learner might base his or her own practice.

The explanation is followed by exercises. For example:

Fill in the blanks in the following and repeat aloud several times:
I make
They . . .
She . . .
The scientist . . .
Scientists . . .   accurate experiments
We . . .
You . . .

And then, after there has been an explanation of the negative:

Fill in the blanks in the following and repeat aloud:
I do not accept
You . . . not accept   incomplete evidence
We . . . not accept   unreliable information
A scientist . . . not accept inaccurate statements
They . . . not accept   authority in science

There then follows an exercise requiring students to put the verbs in brackets into their correct forms, and another which requires them to read sentences off from a substitution table:

An investigator employs complex instruments in his work.
A researcher needs new apparatus in his work. *etc.*

Now which of the different *uses* of the simple present tense that have been explained in the preceding explanation is the student actually realizing here? When they fill in the blanks to produce the expression:

She makes accurate experiments

is this a reference to 'an action in the present which happens usually, habitually or generally' or to a general truth, or to a scientific law, or does it 'describe a process in a general way'?

The answer is, of course, that it does none of these things, because it is simply the composition of a sentence with no indication at all about what its value as an utterance might be. The tense is not being *used* at all: it is just being practised as a linguistic form. The students may have no idea even about the literal meaning of what they compose and repeat. So what, one wonders, is the purpose of the explanation in the first place?

Now it must be noted that the people who are being subjected to such mechanistic exercises are students of science. And they have previously been required to read a passage called 'The Scientific Attitude', the understanding of which presupposes that they already know how this particular tense is used. They could not otherwise be capable of answering the comprehension questions set on it. But the particular point I want to make about this passage is that it gives an eloquent account of the intellectual qualities required of a student of science, which are in absolute contradiction to the unthinking activities that the student is called upon to carry out in the interests of language learning. We are told that the scientist uses 'special methods of thinking and acting' and that he is 'full of curiosity — he wants to find out how the universe works', that he 'directs his attention towards problems', that he is 'highly imaginative', and so on. The students who read this passage will, one assumes, strive to achieve these 'special methods' by the use of curiosity, reason, and imagination, since this is what science learning means. Having been given this glimpse of the scientific attitude that it is desirable that they should adopt, they are then directed to filling in blanks, writing verbs in the correct form, reading off sentences from a substitution table. It is difficult to imagine activities which give less scope for the 'special methods of thinking and acting' which define scientific study.

The explanations, examples, and exercises which are provided in this textbook, and which one supposes are to be applied in the teaching of 'microacts' too, are clearly designed to implant items of knowledge in the learner's mind and not to develop a capacity for using this knowledge. The approach to ESP course design exemplified in this textbook and advocated in Ewer and Boys 1981 is one which is fixated on aims, as defined in the first chapter of this present discussion. It conforms to the Munby principle, and leaves considerations of appropriate methodology entirely out of account.

4. *Schematic types and genre*

Reference was made previously (Discussion 3, Chapter 2) to the general four-part schema proposed by Winter. A search for more specific categories of the same kind, associated with particular kinds of language use, leads to the identification of certain schematic types, which are, as it were, the rhetorical analogues of register (cf. Discussion 5, Chapter 1).

One such attempt to identify more specific schemata is that in Schank and Abelson 1977 (also referred to in Discussion 3, Chapter 2). Here we have the identification of a RESTAURANT-script as consisting of four scenes: entering, ordering, eating, exiting, each one of which can be analysed into further constituents. Such a script constitutes a schematic type.

Another example, with a more direct bearing on ESP, is provided in a recent paper by Swales, which deals with the schematic structure of introductions to journal articles (Swales 1981a). This too is typified by four parts, referred to as 'moves' (cf. the 'scenes' of Schank and Abelson). These are:

Move 1: Establishing the field
Move 2: Summarizing previous research
Move 3: Preparing for present research
Move 4: Introducing present research.

Each of these moves is then analysed in greater detail. What Swales is able to show is that this type of rhetorical routine is used across a wide variety of different fields of enquiry; that is to say, this general interpersonal schema is associated with a number of ideational schemata which define particular (specific) disciplinary areas: molecular physics, electronics, chemical engineering, neurology, educational psychology, management studies, and so on (see Swales 1981a: 8–9).

Swales refers to his investigation as 'genre specific':

> By *genre* I mean a more or less standardised communicative event with a goal or set of goals mutually understood by the participants in that event ... such studies (i.e. of genre) differ from traditional register or sub-register analysis in the importance they attach to communicative purposes within a communicative setting. (Swales 1981a: 10)

It is not, however, entirely clear just what the term *genre* is meant to cover. The examples that Swales cites of genre analysis include work on surgical reports and legal documents, where the routines are specifically associated with particular frames of reference. But the work of Swales himself in this paper deals with a general routine *abstracted* from particular frames of reference. Furthermore, genre analysis is seen to be not merely a matter of describing schematic types of discourse, in principle independent of different linguistic realizations, but also of establishing typical ways in which they are textualized in English (see Widdowson 1979: Chapter 4; 1981b). It therefore embraces, it would appear, studies that have been done on the rhetorical function of grammatical categories like tense (e.g. Lackstrom, Selinker and Trimble 1970, 1973, Oster 1981) and voice (e.g. Tarone, Dwyer, Gillette, and Icke 1981), of co-ordinate constructions (e.g. Widdowson 1973: 8.4) and of participles (e.g. Swales 1981b).

It would seem, then, that the aim of genre analysis is to establish schematic types of both an interpersonal and an ideational kind (routines, frames of reference, routines with frames of reference) and their typical textualization in English. The value of such analysis is that it provides a characterization of the communicative conventions associated with particular areas of language use and takes us beyond the itemization of notions and functions into larger schematic units upon which procedural work can effectively operate. The danger of such analysis is that in revealing typical textualizations, it might lead us to suppose that form-function correlations are fixed and can be learned as formulae, and so to minimize the importance of the procedural aspect of language use and learning.

5. *Procedural types and cognitive style*

I have represented interpretative procedures as problem solving activities. People set about solving problems in different ways, by engaging different mental dispositions or cognitive styles.

It has been suggested that the kind of problem that confronts the learner of a second language is more effectively solved by a 'field-independent' rather than a 'field-dependent' style of thinking, so that the adoption of this style is a feature of 'the good language learner' (see Naiman, Frohlich, and Stern 1975); and other researchers have considered what the cognitive characteristics of effective language learning *in general* might be (Rubin 1975, 1981, Brown 1977, Rogers 1979; see also McDonough 1981: 130–3).

What does not seem to have been considered is the possibility that different styles may be associated more specifically with types of problem which characterize different areas of enquiry and activity, and which define the purposes for which the language is being learned. Hudson, for example, suggests that people who pursue scientific studies incline to thinking of a more convergent kind, whereas the thinking patterns of those who study the arts tend to be divergent (Hudson 1967). Since both groups are presumably equally effective in the use of language for their particular concerns, one might reasonably doubt whether there is one cognitive style generally favourable to language learning. It would seem more reasonable to suppose that learning will be effectively promoted if the learner engages the particular style suited to his or her extra-linguistic purpose.

How far it is possible to characterize different purposes by appeal to the concept of cognitive style must at the moment be a matter for surmise. But clearly if we could do so, then it would be possible to define more closely the kind of procedural work appropriate to particular groups of ESP learners. Just as research on genre, or schematic type, as referred to in the previous discussion, promises to contribute to more effective course design, so would research on cognitive style, or procedural style, characteristic of particular purposes, have potential significance for the devising of appropriate methodology. (For general discussion of this point see Widdowson 1981b.)

Research on 'the good language learner' seeks to identify cognitive styles with the general psychological process of learning. One can consider the question too from a sociological perspective, and seek to identify cognitive styles which appear to typify different cultural patterns of thinking. We enter here the field of contrastive rhetoric, and cognitive style becomes a matter of what Kaplan calls 'cultural thought patterns' (Kaplan 1972). In this paper, Kaplan provides evidence from the written work of students from different cultural backgrounds in support of the proposition:

> Logic (in the popular, rather than the logician's sense of the word), which is the basis of rhetoric, is evolved out of a culture; it is not universal. Rhetoric, then, is not universal either, but varies from culture to culture and even from time to time within a given culture. (Kaplan 1972: 246)

What I have called (Widdowson 1979: Chapter 4) the secondary cultures of different areas of training and education can also be seen to be rhetorically varied. Not only do they require the learning of typical schematic structures (as noted in the previous Discussion) but the actual learning of these structures and the activity of actualizing them must, I would argue, engage procedures which realize the 'cultural thought patterns' or cognitive styles typical of particular areas of enquiry and practice. Thus, to learn to be an engineer must involve an initiation into ways of thinking and behaving which define that secondary sub-culture, and the use of language in this initiation is bound to conform to these sub-cultural conventions. The argument leads us back again to the importance of accounting for procedural activity by means of appropriate methodology.

4 In conclusion

Throughout this book I have been seeking to investigate the issues that are raised by the idea of ESP. My contention is that such an idea, seemingly straightforward enough, reveals under scrutiny quite complex implications about the nature of language and the educational process. If one is going to teach courses of English (or any other language for that matter) for specific purposes, one should be clear just how the notions *English* (or *language*) and *purpose* are to be defined, and what exactly it means to be specific. I do not think, on the whole, that these matters have been given the consideration they deserve. There has been a good deal of attention given to the description of areas of language use and the needs of learners, but much less attention given to the crucial prior question of what exactly it is that is being described. There are those who talk of the lack of research in ESP as if this were simply a matter of amassing quantities of data about the superficial features of varieties of language use without enquiring into what the nature of language use might be. There are others who insist on the importance of needs analysis without investigating the educational implications of such insistence.

The idea of ESP provokes questions of a fundamental and theoretical kind about the definition of learning purpose and language use. In Chapter 1, which deals with the former, I have tried to relate the question of purpose to the concepts of training and education, and to indicate the importance of distinguishing between aims as eventual behavioural targets and objectives, which are the pedagogic constructs designed to facilitate learning and to develop a capacity in the learners for achieving such aims for themselves. Specificity can then be seen as the degree of correspondence between objectives and aims. It follows that the closer the correspondence, the more specific the course and the less scope there will be for individual initiative. Specificity, then, is in inverse proportion to educational value. This does not mean that it is necessarily to be rejected. There will obviously be occasions when

an educational emphasis would be misplaced, where the requirement is for the occupational use of the language for training in the
exercise of vocational skills. It would seem likely, however, that
specificity is a suspect notion in relation to *academic* purposes,
where students must be prepared to use their own initiative to solve
problems which do not fit neatly into prescribed formulae.

How the relationship between formula and problem is to be
represented is a question of general educational concern, and how
it is answered will determine pedagogic objectives. But, as I argue
in Chapter 2, the relationship is essentially the same as that which
holds between a knowledge of language and the way this knowledge is actualized in instances of language use. In both cases, what
concerns us is the way knowledge structures in the mind are
realized as behaviour, the way procedural activity mediates between what we know and what we do. With respect to language
knowledge, I suggested that the formulae were organized on two
levels: the systemic and the schematic, the former representing
linguistic competence, and the latter communicative competence.
Interpretative procedures are required to draw systemic knowledge
into the immediate executive level of schemata and to relate these
schemata to actual instances. The ability to realize particular
meanings, solve particular problems, by relating them to schematic
formulae stored as knowledge, constitutes what I called capacity.

Capacity, then, can be understood as the ability to solve problems and, equivalently, to make meanings by interpreting a particular instance (an event, an expression) as related to some formula,
thereby assimilating the instance into a pre-existing pattern of
knowledge, or, when necessary, by modifying the available formulae so that the instance can be accommodated within them. In this
way, capacity works both to exploit existing competence and also
to extend that competence to make provision for creativity and
change. Capacity so defined is the driving force behind both the
acquisition and the use of language.

The view I am putting forward, then, is that the concepts of
competence as a set of formulae, and capacity as the mediating
force which associates them with actual instances, are not restricted
to matters of language alone. They are conceived of as principles
which control all learning and all uses of learning and which
underlie human conceptual and perceptual processes in general. So
it is that the discussion of learning purpose in Chapter 1 and the
discussion of language use in Chapter 2 converge on the same
issues. The definition of formulae in relation to pedagogic objec-

tives turns out to be basically the same thing as the definition of schemata in relation to language use, and in both cases there is a need to postulate procedures which will realize or actualize knowledge structures as behaviour.

The central task of teaching is to activate these procedures. We come now to Chapter 3. I suggested that ESP course design might be fashioned from schematic units derived from areas of use which students would recognize as having relevance to their concerns. This would not necessarily involve the selection of topics specific to their aims for learning. The important point is that the course content should be such as to engage the students' interest, since not otherwise will they authenticate the language presented as meaningful use by the application of procedures for making sense. The activation of these procedures was, I argued, the basic business of methodology, whose central concern was to stimulate problem solving activities of the kind which were congruent with the students' specialist preoccupations and for which the language was needed as a contingency. Thus methodology was placed at the very heart of the operation, with course design directed at servicing its requirements and not the reverse. In this view, course design is not determined by eventual aims but decided on by reference to pedagogic objectives. It matters less that a course should incorporate the language of a specific purpose than that the language it contains should lead to purposeful activity. The whole teaching enterprise is seen not as the inculcation of a limited competence by whatever contrivance is most readily available, but as the development of a capacity in the students for using the language so that they can achieve their own competence and their own purposes.

Over the preceding three chapters I have been trying to define ESP in relation to a number of conceptual distinctions. To summarize, I have been saying this: an ESP enterprise has to be located on a scale of specificity which in effect controls the degree of equivalence between objectives and aims. Training appears towards one end of this scale and education towards the other. A shift in orientation towards specificity brings objectives into closer alignment with aims. This narrows the distance between schemata and active use, and equivalently between formula and problem. And this in turn leads to a diminution in the role of methodology, understood as a set of activities designed to develop the procedural problem solving capacity of learners. This capacity carries over into the achievement of aims through learning after the course is over. Perhaps there are trainees whose needs can be accounted for by limiting them to the restricted competence of a formulaic pattern of linguistic behaviour, but not all learners, and particularly not those whose very purposes are educational, can or should be confined in this way. It should be recognized that such confinement, no matter how justified it may be on other grounds, runs counter to educational principles.

All this may seem excessively elaborate — a glass bead game of over-nice distinctions remote from the reality of practical teaching. But I do not see that anything less complex can provide us with the essential conceptual bearings we need to locate and describe ESP as an area of language education. We cannot do otherwise than to consider the nature of language and of education, and the relationship that holds between them.

There are two general points of significance that should be apparent from the arguments and discussions in these chapters. First, the learning of language, like the learning of anything else, is a matter of relating knowledge abstracted from past experience as systems, schemata, formulae, to actual instances by procedural, problem solving activity. Competence and capacity are not uniquely concerned with language. Secondly, and as a corollary, the criteria that have to be thought about and thought through in course design and methodology for the teaching of language for use derive from principles of general pedagogy and are not exclusive to language teaching.

What bearing do these points have on ESP in particular? They indicate, I think, that the learning of language for a purpose cannot be dissociated from the other activities that need to be undertaken to achieve that purpose. The English to be learned can be purposeful only to the extent that the activities it is used for are purposeful in the actual learning process. But this is true of all language teaching which seeks to develop the ability to cope with language as a means of conceptualization and communication. What then is so special or specific about ESP? We return to the question posed at the very beginning of this book.

In ESP we are dealing with students for whom the learning of English is auxiliary to some other primary professional or academic purpose. It is clearly a means for achieving something else and is not an end in itself; and that something else has been independently formulated as a set of aims, and any course of instruction designed with these in mind will have established its own appropriate objectives accordingly. This being so, ESP is (or ought logically to be) integrally linked with areas of activity (academic, vocational, professional) which have already been defined and which represent the learners' aspirations. The learning of ESP is in consequence an essentially *dependent* activity, a parasitic process, and it follows that the pedagogy of ESP must be dependent too. It has no purposes of its own; it exists only to service those that have been specified elsewhere.

It is this inherently dependent nature of ESP that distinguishes it from general purpose English (GPE). GPE has somehow to create the conditions for its own existence as a school subject; it has to make provision for learners who have no particular aim in view beyond the end of the course. This means that its objectives have to be independently formulated and the necessary purposeful activity is in consequence more difficult to achieve. Whereas in ESP, which has no separate subject status, it is a matter of exploiting the opportunity afforded by already existing purposes, in general purpose English it is a matter of creating purposes out of nothing by pedagogic invention. But in both cases, these purposes must be such as to engage the learner's use of procedures for realizing schematic meaning, drawing on his or her knowledge of the language system as a resource. Both exploitation and invention depend on a prior understanding of the nature of learning purpose and language use and the way they are related. We return again to the main point.

When I set out to write this book, my intention was to investigate, with as much rigour as I could muster, the substructure of assumption that supports the very extensive institutional edifice of ESP. This investigation has led me to a consideration, in some detail, of issues in education and the theory of language, simply because such issues revealed themselves as soon as the assumptions were subjected to scrutiny. I did not seek them out; they came of their own accord.

It might be objected that I have not dealt with the particular practical problems that the ESP teacher is faced with — problems which call for immediate administrative decisions about what and how to teach, and which allow little leisure for indulgence in theoretical speculation. But such decisions cannot be dealt with in advance: all one can do is to indicate the kinds of consideration that they need to take into account. To the extent that they are informed by principle and not merely controlled by expediency, these decisions must depend on the teacher taking bearings on the theoretical issues that I have been raising here. Where compromises are called for to accommodate local constraints, they can be based only on an understanding of how the principles of language teaching pedagogy are being compromised.

Theory, then, is of benefit to ESP, even, perhaps particularly, in its most practical manifestations. But ESP is also of benefit to theory. It confronts us with problems which challenge us to question the established formulae of conventional thinking. ESP, in this sense, provides us with the opportunity to further our own education as language teachers, whether we are concerned with specific purposes or not, and to reappraise the principles and practices of language teaching in general.

References

Allwright, R. L. 1977. 'Language learning through communication practice'. *ELT Documents* 76/3 (reprinted in Brumfit and Johnson 1979).

Allwright, R. L. 1979. 'Abdication and responsibility in language teaching'. *Studies in Second Language Acquisition*, Vol. 2 No. 1.

Altman, H. B. and **C. V. James** (eds.). 1980. *Foreign Language Teaching: Meeting Individual Needs*. Oxford: Pergamon.

Bartlett, F. C. 1932. *Remembering*. Cambridge: Cambridge University Press.

Beaugrande, R. de. 1980. *Text, Discourse and Process*. London: Longman.

Beaugrande, R. de and **W. Dressler.** 1981. *Introduction to Text Linguistics*. London: Longman.

Bloom, B. S. (ed.). 1972. *Taxonomy of Educational Objectives*. London: Longman.

Bobrow, D. and **A. Collins** (eds.). 1975. *Representation and Understanding: Studies in Cognitive Science*. New York: Academic Press.

Bransford, J. D. and **M. K. Johnson.** 1972. 'Contextual prerequisites for understanding: some investigations of comprehension and recall'. *Journal of Verbal Learning and Verbal Behaviour* Vol. 11.

Brown, H. D. 1977. 'Cognitive and affective characteristics of good language learners'. Second Language Research Forum, University of California at Los Angeles, February 1977.

Brown, P. and **S. Levinson.** 1978. 'Universals in language usage: politeness phenomena' in Goody 1978.

Brumfit, C. J. 1979. 'Accuracy and fluency as polarities in foreign language teaching'. *Bulletin CILA* 29.

Brumfit, C. J. 1980. *Problems and Principles in English Teaching*. Oxford: Pergamon.

Brumfit, C. J. 1981. 'Linguistic specifications for fluency work:

how meaningful a question?' in Richtertich and Widdowson 1981.

Brumfit, C. J. and **K. Johnson** (eds.). 1979. *The Communicative Approach to Language Teaching.* Oxford: Oxford University Press.

Cheong, Lee Kok. 1978. *Syntax of Scientific English.* Singapore: Singapore University Press.

Chomsky, N. 1965. *Aspects of the Theory of Syntax.* Cambridge, Mass: MIT Press.

Cicourel, A. 1973. *Cognitive Sociology.* Harmondsworth: Penguin.

Clark, H. H. and **S. E. Haviland.** 1977. 'Comprehension and the given-new contract' in Freedle 1977.

Cole, P. and **J. Morgan** (eds.). 1975. *Syntax and Semantics III: Speech Acts.* New York: Academic Press.

Corder, S. P. 1967. 'The significance of learners' errors'. *IRAL* Vol. V No. 4. (Reprinted in Richards 1974 and Corder 1981.)

Corder, S. P. 1981. *Error Analysis and Interlanguage.* Oxford: Oxford University Press.

Coulthard, R. M. 1977. *An Introduction to Discourse Analysis.* London: Longman.

Croft K. (ed.). 1972. *Readings in English as a Second Language.* Cambridge: Winthrop.

Crystal, D. and **D. Davy.** 1969. *Investigating English Style.* London: Longman.

Dakin, J., B. Tiffen, and **H. G. Widdowson.** 1968. *Language in Education: The Problems in Commonwealth Africa and the Indo-Pakistan Sub-Continent.* London: Oxford University Press.

van Dijk, T. 1977a. *Text and Context.* London: Longman.

van Dijk, T. 1977b. 'Semantic macro-structures and knowledge frames in discourse comprehension' in Just and Carpenter 1977.

Dooling, D. J. and **R. Lachman.** 1971. 'Effects of comprehension on retention of prose'. *Journal of Experimental Psychology,* Vol. 88.

van Ek, J. A. 1975. *The Threshold Level.* Strasbourg: Council of Europe. (Reprinted 1980, Oxford: Pergamon.)

Ewer, J. R. 1981. 'Nine problem areas in ESP'. *English for Specific Purposes,* No. 54. Corvallis: Oregon State University.

Ewer, J. R. and **O. Boys.** 1981. 'The EST textbook situation: an enquiry'. *The ESP Journal* Vol. 1 No. 2.

Ewer, J. R. and G. Hughes-Davies. 1971. 'Further notes on developing an ELT programme for students of science and technology'. *ELT Journal* Vol. XXVI No. 1.

Ewer, J. R. and G. Latorre. 1967. 'Preparing an English course for students of science'. *ELT Journal* Vol. XXI No. 3.

Ewer, J. R. and G. Latorre. 1969. *A Course in Basic Scientific English*. London: Longman.

Fillenbaum, S. 1973. *Syntactic Factors in Memory*. The Hague: Mouton.

Firth, J. R. 1957. *Papers in Linguistics 1934–1951*. London: Oxford University Press.

Fisher, J.C., M.A. Clarke, and J. Schachter (eds.). 1981. *On TESOL '80: Building Bridges*. Washington DC: TESOL.

Freedle, R.O. (ed.). 1977. *Discourse Production and Comprehension*. Norwood, New Jersey: Ablex.

Garfinkel, H. 1972. 'Remarks on ethnomethodology' in Gumperz and Hymes 1972.

Garfinkel, H. and H. Sacks. 1970. 'On formal structures of practical actions' in McKinney and Tiryakan 1970.

Goody, E.N. (ed.). 1978. *Questions and Politeness: Strategies in Social Interaction*. Cambridge: Cambridge University Press.

Grice, P. 1975. 'Logic and conversation' in Cole and Morgan 1975.

Gumperz, J. and D. Hymes (eds.). 1972. *Directions in Sociolinguistics: The Ethnography of Communication*. New York: Holt, Rinehart and Winston.

Halliday, M. A. K. 1973. *Explorations in the Functions of Language*. London: Edward Arnold.

Halliday, M. A. K. 1979. *Language as Social Semiotic*. London: Edward Arnold.

Halliday, M. A. K. and R. Hasan. 1976. *Cohesion in English*. London: Longman.

Halliday, M. A. K., P. Strevens, and A. McIntosh. 1964. *The Linguistic Sciences and Language Teaching*. London: Oxford University Press.

Hatch, E. M. (ed.). 1978. *Second Language Acquisition: A Book of Readings*. Rowley, Mass: Newbury House.

Heritage, J. C. and D. R. Watson. 1979. 'Formulations as conversational objects' in Psathas 1979.

Hinde, R. A. (ed.). 1972. *Non-verbal Communication*. London: Oxford University Press.

Hoey, M. 1979. 'Signalling in discourse'. *Discourse Analysis Monographs* No. 6. University of Birmingham: English Language Research.

Holec, H. 1980. *Autonomy and Foreign Language Learning.* Strasbourg: Council of Europe.

Howatt, A. P. 1984. *A History of English Language Teaching.* Oxford: Oxford University Press.

Huddleston, R. D., R. A. Hudson, E. O. Winter, and A. Henrici. 1968. *Sentence and Clause in Scientific English.* London: Communication Research Centre, University College London.

Hudson, L. 1967. *Contrary Imaginations.* Harmondsworth: Penguin.

Hutchinson, T. and **A. Waters.** 1980a. 'ESP at the crossroads'. *English for Specific Purposes,* No. 36. Corvallis: Oregon State University.

Hutchinson, T. and **A. Waters.** 1980b. 'Communication in the technical classroom'. *ELT Documents* Special Issue. London: The British Council.

Hutchinson, T. and **A. Waters.** 1981. 'Performance and competence in ESP'. *Applied Linguistics,* Vol. II No. 1.

Hymes, D. 1972. 'On communicative competence' in Pride and Holmes 1972.

Hymes, D. 1974. *Foundations in Sociolinguistics.* Philadelphia: University of Pennsylvania Press.

Illich, I. 1970. *Deschooling Society.* New York: Harper and Row.

Jefferson, G. 1972. 'Side sequences' in Sudnow 1972.

Just, M. A. and **P. A. Carpenter** (eds.). 1977. *Cognitive Processes in Comprehension.* Hillsdale, New Jersey: Erlbaum.

Kaplan, R. B. 1972. 'Cultural thought patterns in inter-cultural education' in Croft 1972.

Krashen, S. D. 1981. *Second Language Acquisition and Second Language Learning.* Oxford: Pergamon

Krashen, S. D. 1982. *Principles and Practice in Second Language Aquisition:* Oxford: Pergamon.

Labov, W. and **D. Fanshel.** 1977. *Therapeutic Discourse.* New York: Academic Press.

Lackstrom, J., L. Selinker, and **L. Trimble.** 1970. 'Grammar and technical English' in Lugton 1970.

Lackstrom, J., L. Selinker, and L. Trimble. 1973. 'Technical rhetorical principles and grammatical choice'. *TESOL Quarterly*, No. 7.

Lakoff, R. 1973. 'The logic of politeness: or minding your p's and q's'. Papers from the ninth regional meeting of the Chicago Linguistics Society.

Leech, G. N. 1977. 'Language and tact'. *LAUT* (University of Trier), Series A, Paper 46.

Leech, G. N. 1981. *Semantics* (2nd. edn.). Harmondsworth: Penguin.

Levelt, W. J. M. 1975. 'Skill theory and language teaching'. *Studies in Second Language Acquisition*, Vol. 1 No. 1.

Lugton, R. C. (ed.). 1970. *English as a Second Language in Current Issues*. Philadelphia: Centre for Curriculum Development.

Lyons, J. 1972. 'Human language' in Hinde 1972.

Lyons, J. 1977. *Semantics* I and II. Cambridge: Cambridge University Press.

Mackey, W. F. 1965. *Language Teaching Analysis*. London: Longman.

McDonough, S. H. 1981. *Psychology in Foreign Language Teaching*. London: George Allen and Unwin.

McKinney, J. C. and E. A. Tiryakian (eds.). 1970. *Theoretical Sociology*. New York: Appleton Century Crofts.

Magee, B. 1973. *Popper*. London: Fontana/Collins.

Morris, I. 1954. *The Art of Teaching English as a Living Language*. London: Macmillan.

Munby, J. 1978. *Communicative Syllabus Design*. 1978. Cambridge: Cambridge University Press.

Naiman, N., M. Frohlich, and H. H. Stern. 1975. *The Good Language Learner*. Toronto: Ontario Institute for Studies in Education.

Neisser, U. 1976. *Cognition and Reality*. San Francisco: W. H. Freeman.

Oster, S. 1981. 'The use of tenses in "reporting past literature" in EST' in Selinker, Tarone and Hanzeli 1981.

Palmer, F. R. 1968. *Selected Papers of J. R. Firth 1952–1959*. London: Longman.

Palmer, H. E. 1964. *The Principles of Language Study.* London: Oxford University Press. (First published 1922.)

Pask, G. and **B. C. E. Scott.** 1972. 'Learning strategies and individual competence'. *International Journal of Man-Machine Studies,* No. 4.

Peters, R. S. (ed.). 1967. *The Concept of Education.* London: Routledge and Kegan Paul.

Peters, R. S. 1973a. 'Aims of education: a conceptual enquiry' in Peters 1973b.

Peters, R. S. (ed.). 1973b. *The Philosophy of Education.* London: Oxford University Press.

Piaget, J. 1953. *The Origins of Intelligence in the Child.* London: Routledge and Kegan Paul.

Piaget, J. 1955. *The Child's Construction of Reality.* London: Routledge and Kegan Paul.

Popper, K. 1972. *Objective Knowledge.* Oxford: Oxford University Press.

Pride, J. B. and **J. Holmes** (eds.). 1972. *Sociolinguistics: Selected Readings.* Harmondsworth: Penguin.

Psathas, G. (ed.). 1979. *Everyday Language: Studies in Ethnomethodology.* New York: Irvington.

Richards, J. C. (ed.). 1974. *Error Analysis: Perspectives on Second Language Acquisition.* London: Longman.

Richterich, R. 1973. *Systems Development in Adult Language Learning.* Strasbourg: Council of Europe. (Republished: Richterich, R. and J-L. Chancerel. 1980. *Identifying the Needs of Adults Learning a Foreign Language.* Oxford: Pergamon.)

Richterich, R. and **H. G. Widdowson** (eds.). 1981. *Description, présentation et enseignement des langues.* Paris: Credif Hatier.

Robinson, P. 1980. *ESP (English for Specific Purposes).* Oxford: Pergamon.

Rodgers, T. S. 1979. 'Towards a model of learner variation in autonomous language learning'. *Studies in Second Language Acquisition,* Vol. 2 No. 1.

Rubin, J. 1975. 'What the "good language learner" can teach us'. *TESOL Quarterly,* No. 9.

Rubin, J. 1981. 'Study of cognitive processes in language learning'. *Applied Linguistics,* Vol. II No. 2.

Ryle, G. 1967. 'Teaching and training' in Peters 1967.

Sacks, H. 1972. 'On the analysability of stories by children' in Gumperz and Hymes 1972.

Sacks, H. 1979. 'Hotrodder: a revolutionary category' in Psathas 1979.

Sanford, A. J. and S. C. Garrod. 1981. *Understanding Written Discourse: Explorations in Comprehension Beyond the Sentence.* Chichester: John Wiley.

Schank, R. and R. Abelson. 1977. *Scripts, Plans, Goals and Understanding.* Hillsdale, New Jersey: Erlbaum.

Searle, J. R. 1969. *Speech Acts.* Cambridge: Cambridge University Press.

Searle, J. R. 1979. *Expression and Meaning.* Cambridge: Cambridge University Press.

Selinker, L., E. Tarone, and V. Hanzeli (eds.). 1981. *English For Academic and Technical Purposes: Studies in Honor of Louis Trimble.* Rowley, Mass: Newbury House.

Selinker, L., L. Trimble, and M. T. Trimble. 1978. 'Rhetorical function shifts in EST discourse'. *TESOL Quarterly*, No. 12.

Sinclair, J. McH., and R. M. Coulthard. 1975. *Towards an Analysis of Discourse.* London: Oxford University Press.

Smith, F. 1978. *Reading.* Cambridge: Cambridge University Press.

Smith, N. and D. Wilson. 1979. *Modern Linguistics.* Harmondsworth: Penguin.

Strevens, P. D. 1980. *Teaching English as an International Language.* Oxford: Pergamon.

Sudnow, D. (ed.). 1972. *Studies in Social Interaction.* New York: The Free Press.

Swales, J. 1981a. 'Aspects of article introductions'. *Aston ESP Research Reports* No. 1. Language Studies Unit, The University of Aston in Birmingham.

Swales, J. 1981b. 'The function of one type of particle in a chemistry textbook' in Selinker, Tarone, and Hanzeli 1981.

Swales, J. 1983. *Episodes in ESP.* Oxford: Pergamon.

Tarone, E., S. Dwyer, S. Gillette, and V. Icke. 1981. 'The use of the passive in two Astrophysics Journal papers'. *The ESP Journal*, Vol. 1 No. 2.

Trim, J. L. M. 1980. 'The place of needs analysis in the Council of Europe Modern Languages Project' in Altman and James 1980.

Tyler, S. A. 1969. *Cognitive Anthropology.* New York: Holt, Rinehart, and Winston.

Werth, P. 1981. *Conversation and Discourse.* London: Croom Helm.

West, M. (ed.). 1953. *A General Service List of English Words.* London: Longman.

Widdowson, H. G. 1968. 'The teaching of English through science' in Dakin, Tiffen, and Widdowson 1968.

Widdowson, H. G. 1973. 'An applied linguistic approach to discourse analysis'. Unpublished Ph. D. thesis, University of Edinburgh.

Widdowson, H. G. 1975. *Stylistics and the Teaching of Literature.* London: Longman.

Widdowson, H. G. 1978. *Teaching Language as Communication.* London: Oxford University Press.

Widdowson, H. G. 1979. *Explorations in Applied Linguistics.* London: Oxford University Press.

Widdowson, H. G. 1980. 'Models and fictions'. *Applied Linguistics*, Vol. I No. 2.

Widdowson, H. G. 1981a. 'ESP: the curse of Caliban' in Fisher, Clarke, and Schachter 1981.

Widdowson, H. G. 1981b. 'English for specific purposes: criteria for course design' in Selinker, Tarone, and Hanzeli 1981.

Wilkins, D. A. 1976. *Notional Syllabuses.* London: Oxford University Press.

Wilson, D. and **D. Sperber.** 1981. 'On Grice's theory of conversation' in Werth 1981.

Winter, E. O. 1971. 'Connection in science material'. *Papers and Reports* No. 7. London: Centre for Information on Language Teaching.

Winter, E. O. 1976. 'Fundamentals of Information Structure'. Hatfield Polytechnic (mimeo).

Winter, E. O. 1977. 'A clause relational approach to English texts'. Special issue of *Instructional Science*, Vol. 6.

Index

abilities, 17–18
acceptability, 78–9
  procedures, 48
accessibility, 78–9
accommodation, 67
adjacency pair, 75–7
aims, 6–7
  and course design, 82–3
  and learner needs, 20–3
  and objectives, 12, 20–1, 31,
    32–3, 80–1, 83–5, 90–1
  and register analysis, 33
ambiguity, 36, 59–61
assimilation, 67
  questions, 82
authenticity, 30

Bloom, B. S., 21–2
Boys, O., 95
Bransford, J. D., 72
Brown, P., 78

capacity, 7–8, 17, 23–8, 67, 106
  relationship with competence, 11
Chomsky, N., 26, 38, 39
Cicourel, A., 68, 70–1
Clark, H. H., 68–9, 70–1
clause-relations, 73
cognitive style, 102–4
coherence, 69–71
collocation, 65
communication, 30–1
  and schemata, 40
communicative categories, 30–1
communicative competence, 7–8
  definition, 23–5
  and needs analysis, 10
communicative operations, 95
communicative skill, 17–18
competence, 7–8, 23–8, 106

relation with capacity, 11
comprehension questions, 82, 92
connotation, 65
co-operative imperative, 47, 78–9
co-operative principle, 62, 63, 68
  routine procedures and, 74, 75
Corder, S. P., 26
Coulthard, R. M., 75–6
course design, 12, 80–104, 107–8
  and purpose, 9
  historical perspectives, 14–16
courses
  'narrow-angle', 81
  'wide-angle', 81
creativity, 8
cultural thought patterns, 103

decontextualization, 51
van Dijk, T., 55–6, 77–8
discourse
  and schemata, 37
  coherence in, 69–71
  literary, 37
  structure, 58
discrimination questions, 82
Dooling D. J., 72

education, 80
  and language, 80–1
  'pure', 19
  and training, 16–20
English for Academic Purposes
  (EAP), 9
English for Occupational Purposes
  (EOP), 9
English for Specific Purposes (ESP),
  5–6, 107–10
  development, 16
  historical perspectives, 14–16
  methodology, 87–91, 95–100

'narrow-angle' courses, 81, 89, 90
objectives and aims, 12–13
subdivisions, 9
textbooks, 96, 97–9
'wide-angle' courses, 81, 89–91
error, 27
Ewer, J. R., 93–4, 95–6, 98
expansions, 71, 77

face-threatening acts, 78
Fanshel, D., 75
Fillenbaum, S., 60
Firth, J. R., 28, 57
formulae, 106
formulations, 46, 77–8
frames of reference, 37, 39, 41, 55–6, 59, 63
and procedures, 42–3, 67–74, 77
function words, 94

Garfinkel, H., 68
Garrod, S. C., 57, 61
general purpose English (GPE), 5–6
nature of, 109
genre, 101–2
gist, formulation of, 46, 77
Grice, P., 68

Halliday, M. A. K., 28, 38, 39, 56
Haviland, S. E., 68–9, 70–1
Hutchinson, T., 93–4
Hymes, D., 23, 56–7

idealization, 50–2
ideational schemata, 55, 63, 69
illocutionary act, 43
illocutionary intent, 48, 49, 74
indexical meaning, 60–1, 62, 63
indices, 52
interpersonal schemata, 55–7, 74, 76
interpretative procedures, 70–3
and schemata, 40–6

Johnson, M. K., 72

Kaplan, R. B., 103

Krashen, S. D., 27

Labov, W., 75
Lachman, R., 72
Lackstrom, J., 58
language acquisition, 38, 39
device (LAD), 26
language functions and course design, 87
language learner, good, 102–3
language learning, 108
aims, 12
language teaching, historical perspectives, 14–16
language use, idealizations, 32–3
language-forming capacity, 26
languages, restricted, 29
learner needs, and aims and objectives, 20–3
learning, 18
needs, 20–1
Levinson, S., 78
linguistic competence, 7–8, 25, 35
and course design, 82
and register analysis, 9
linguistic skill, 17
logical sequence relation, 73
Lyons, J., 26, 62

McIntosh, A., 28
macro-structures, 77
matching relation, 73
meaning
perception of, 65–7
potential, 17, 27
membership categorization devices, 63
metaphor, 41, 62–5
methodology, 87–91, 95–100, 107
'microacts', 95, 96–7
Morris, I., 14
Munby, J., 20–1, 52–3, 86, 95–6

needs analysis, 9–10, 20–2, 28–9
and course design, 33, 85–7
Neisser, U., 65–7

objectives, 6–7
and aims, 12, 20–1, 31, 32–3,

80–1, 83–5, 90–1
and course design, 82–3
and learner needs, 20–3
and register analysis, 33

Palmer, H. E., 14, 15, 26, 27
perception, 65–7
perceptual cycle, 66
Peters, R. S., 16–19
plan, 56
pragmatic normalization, 60
presentation, communicative
approach to, 81–2
procedural negotiation, 45
procedural vocabulary, 92–5
procedures, 40–50, 88–9
acceptability, 48
co-operative, 47
frames of reference, 42–3
interpretative, 40–6, 70–3
and language skills, 86
protective, 48–9
and rhetorical routines, 43–5
routine, 74–7
types, 102–4
propositional content
and frames of reference, 37, 49
protective procedures, 48–9
purpose, 6
and course design, 9
learning, 5–31

questions
assimilation, 82
comprehension, 82, 92
discrimination, 82
reference, 82

reading, 61
reference questions, 82
register analysis, 9, 28–9, 84
and course design, 32–3
restricted languages, 29
rhetorical process chart, 58–9
rhetorical routines, 37, 41, 58, 101
and procedures, 43–5
Robinson, P., 15
routine, 57
procedures, 74–7
Ryle, G., 18–19

Sacks, H., 71, 75
Sanford, A. J., 57, 61
scenario, 57, 58
schemata, 34–40, 54–9
and course design, 81–2, 88
and language functions, 87
and procedures, 40–50
ideational, 55, 63, 69
interpersonal, 55, 56, 57, 74, 76
prospective function, 65
types, 101–2
schematic anticipation, 61–2
schematic projections, 61
schematic vocabulary, 94
scientific English, 96
script, 56–7
Selinker, L., 58
sentence
ambiguity, 36
connectors, 73
side sequence, 77
situational presentation, 81–2
skills, 17–18
itemization, 52–4
language and course design,
86–7
learning, 30
specificity, 105–6
speech
event, 56–7
situation, 56–7
Strevens, P. D., 15, 28
structural syllabuses
and learner needs, 20
word counts in, 94–5
Swales, J., 101–2
symbols, 51

tautology, 62–5
taxonomy, 54
teachability, 95
teaching, 18
technical language, 93
territorial imperative, 47, 78–9
topics, 85, 91
training, 8, 10, 11, 80
and education, 16–20
language, 80
'pure', 19
transition relevance, 76

Trim, J. L. M., 22
Trimble, L., 58
Trimble, M. T., 58
Tyler, S. A., 54

upshot, formulation of, 46, 77
utterance ambiguity, 36

verbal art, 27

vocabulary
'common-core', 84, 92–3
procedural, 92–5
schematic, 94

Waters, A., 93–4
Winter, E. O., 58, 73–4
word counts, 94